RACING YESTERDAY

Andy Baxter

"Why should you row a boat race?
Why endure the long months of pain in preparation for a fierce
half hour that will leave you all but dead?
Does anyone ask the question?
Is there anyone who would not go through all the costs, and more,
for the moment when anguish breaks into triumph
or even for the glory of having nobly lost?
Is life less than a boat race?
If a man will give the blood in his body to win the one,
will he not spend all the might of his soul to prevail in the other?"

— Oliver Wendell Holmes, Jr.

Acknowledgements...

Acknowledgements are a slippery slope,
like standing on the edge of a snow laden cornice.
Once you start thanking folks you think of more folks to thank,
and once you get caught up in thanking folks you
stress over the folks you may have forgotten.
So let's do this - everyone who is mentioned in this book;
consider this your acknowledgement and your tribute,
and know that it is *heartfelt.*

Now on to those not mentioned – for the book itself,
*Amy Belki*n for her passion in dissecting this mass of stuff,
Robert Frost for his professionalism as a graphic artist,
Stephany Evans for taking me on as a client and going the long haul,
Barb Barasa for her ruthless integrity in all things website media.

Outside of the book itself I would have to thank
Ken Morrish, Dan Smith, John Rodriguez, Ed Taaffe, Joe Smith
and *Gary Shields* for teaching me a thing or two about
strength of character.

Finally, I recognize *Mary Sherrill Baxter.*
I am lucky to have had not one, but two great mothers
to look up to, learn from and admire.

– Andy

To see photos of this adventure visit our website:
www.racingyesterday.com

This book is dedicated to my parents, *Gail and Alfred Baxter,*
and my brother and best friend *Eric Baxter.*

FOREWARD by Stephen Kiesling

Years ago I went to a psychiatrist in search of a prescription for Ritalin, the tiny white pills that are supposed to keep hyperactive kids from bouncing off walls. My reason was simple: improving my concentration. Keeping my mind in the boat didn't matter so much when I was rowing for Yale; in fact, I wrote my first book, The Shell Game, from the four seat of the varsity eight. But when I switched to smaller boats, I often had to steer as well as to row, and that was more challenging. To get better, I went to a famous sports psychologist and learned that I was almost off his scale for distractibility. Instead of little white pills, he prescribed brain exercises to sharpen my focus, and I was dutifully practicing one of them during the first heat of the 1984 Olympic trials when we veered off the course and rammed an enormous orange buoy at the 500-meter mark.

So much for that.

Then a friend gave me one of the little white pills, and it seemed to help. So I checked the phonebook and went to a local shrink to get my own. He listened to my stories for a couple of hours, writing furiously on his notepad, and finally he shook his head and said he wouldn't give me Ritalin. Instead, he went to his cupboard and brought out sample boxes of the really big white pills, the ones shaped like tiny submarines without the conning towers.

But why? I asked.

He said I was nuts.

I tried to explain that I am an oarsman; that rowers typically do more before breakfast than most people do in a week. But he wasn't listening. He explained that the big white pills would take away the desire to do silly things. Life would get easier, he promised – as if that was the point. He then gave me a free month's supply to get me started. So I took them home and put them in a drawer. Each time I feel compelled to do something truly silly – like train again for the Olympics at age forty-nine – I open the drawer, look at the pills, remind myself that life is short, and resolve to go ahead and try.

I also know that I am not alone in this kind of thinking. Rowers often seem controlled and well behaved, but look more closely and you'll find them working on strange and wonderful and impossible things. Take my friend Andy Baxter, for example. He's an expert on aging and physical fitness, and he designs state-of-the art gyms and equipment and training programs for people over fifty. He knows what is humanly possible at any age. He also has a family and a mortgage. In other words, his life was already overly full when I asked if he was willing to add something huge and impossible, but he jumped at the chance.

Why? He's an oarsman. Why not?

This is Andy's fine account of our adventure. I wish I could say that we succeeded in winning the trials. But having won and lost many times the thing that is most important is a good story, and this is definitely one of those.

Contents

INTRODUCTION

As a sport, rowing has been around for a while. The longest consistently held athletic event known to man is a rowing race. Although few have heard of the Doggett's Coat and Badge, it began in 1715 and exists to this day, held every July on the Thames River. Rowing is the oldest intercollegiate sport in the United States, with the first race between Yale and Harvard Universities being held August 3, 1852. The Oxford-Cambridge competition, known the world over simply as "The Boat Race," has been pitting Olympic-caliber leviathans against each other since 1829.

When I graduated high school I knew I wanted to row. My friend Andy Rogers was going to Cal Berkeley to row for the Bears as his father, Gary, had done before him. My Uncle Dave Dunlap (not my real uncle, though I didn't know that as a kid) won a gold medal rowing in the 1932 Olympics. His oar hung above the mantle in the Napa, California ranch home that my mom had designed for him and Aunt Elizabeth (not my real Aunt). Uncle Dave had the super human ability to split seemingly un-splittable logs with an axe. I would sit on crunchy brown oak leaves, eat a cheese sandwich and watch, in awe, the mechanics of his act. The same physical properties that made Uncle Dave an Olympic oarsman lend themselves deftly to combating oak with hickory and steel. Uncle Dave swung an axe so well because he was a big, giant lever.

I would get my chance to apply leverage at Humboldt State University, California. Every year, like most colleges with a crew program, HSU would set up one of their shiny rowing shells on the quad as bait, then wait to pounce on anyone over six feet tall who came over to investigate. At 6'5", I was an easy mark, made easier still by the fact that they did not need to recruit me. I was on my way to them with considerable intent.

Like so many other rowers before me, I had participated in various sports prior; cross country as a youth, boxing, soccer, cycling, ultimate Frisbee, triathlon, even a brief and half-hearted stab at football. I have always loved cycling, though I'm too big to be much of a threat in that sport. But here was something, I thought to myself, that I could embrace on myriad levels: power, control, endurance, teamwork, intensity, pain, suffering, challenge and reward. Rowing would define me. My place in the world would be cemented. Rowing would become my home.

I embraced the training. I welcomed the discipline. I shared in the camaraderie. And like so many other rowers before me, I read Stephen Kiesling's *The Shell Game*. In the 293 years since oarsmen first squared off on the Thames, precious few truly great books have been written about rowing. I would argue that one could count all of the truly great books written about rowing in the last 293 years on one hand. I would further argue that, of the books on that one hand, Stephen Kiesling's *The Shell Game* would be among them. Those who know even a little bit about rowing would agree with me. That is what I would argue.

I would not say that rowing is misunderstood any more than it is simply *not* understood. Steve's trials validated our own in the sport, and helped us explain to our loved ones why we did what we did. *You got up at what time in the morning? It was raining? After you regained consciousness and wiped the vomit off your face, you did it again?* It is hard to relate to your peers, your relatives, and your girlfriend/boyfriend, why you would commit to something so wholly engrossing with so little to show for it. In Steve's book we rowers had found a voice. The rowing subculture was already strange and cult like. Anyone who could translate it championed our cause. After Steve's book hit the shelves, we didn't have to stutter and stammer about how rowing builds strength of character and moral fiber, we could simply shove *The Shell Game* into their hands and say, "Read this, then you will understand." Steve was our hero.

After graduating college and moving back to Oakland, California, I was feeling unsettled. Rowing had provided me with structure. Structure was something that I'd rarely had growing up and I craved it. Structure gave me concrete objectives, goals to keep me focused, and a reason to get up at seemingly stupid hours of the morning, which I had always loved as a kid. When I was young, getting up at 5:00 a.m. was not a punishment, but an opportunity to possibly catch Santa between the fireplace and the front door, before my brothers got to him. Getting up at 5:00 a.m. meant a chance to climb into oversized boots and gloves, and then head off through the darkness with my dad in a giant semi-truck bound for Napa's Mt. Veeder. We were in the wine business and when the crush was in full swing our family's Veedercrest Vineyards did not differentiate between night and day. Stemmer-crushers stemmed and crushed, pumps and hoses gurgled and spat, and floodlights and generators ensured that, if there was work to be done, 11:00 p.m. looked just like 11:00 a.m. Little boys sometimes slept under tables to stay out of the way, but were damned sure not going to miss out on the action.

Somehow I had resigned myself to the precept that rowing was a college sport. When college was over, rowing was over. I was living in a big Victorian apartment in a really bad part of town where rent was cheap. Not being able to sleep early one morning (screeching car tires, gunfire, sirens, helicopters, take your pick), I went for a run. The Lake Merritt district was safe by comparison to my gangland digs, so I headed that way, staying on the darker streets so as not to draw attention to myself. Lake Merritt has its wonderful "necklace of lights" draped around the water's edge, providing sufficient illumination for exercisers during the early morning and evening hours. The necklace of lights had been waiting for me, maybe for longer than I knew. It directed me straight to the boathouse of the Lake Merritt Rowing Club.

It turns out that there were others in the world who had been wandering about since college, searching for that something to fill a void, and some had found that thing in masters rowing. I came upon a group of half dressed men standing in the boathouse parking lot at 4:50 in the morning. That could only mean one thing: they had all been mugged and were too embarrassed to come out of the shadows, or they were rowers. That's two things. They were rowers. This was a rowing club. Yes, I could join them. I was home. Different family members and a different house, but home just the same. I got back to the practice of applying leverage.

Millions of strokes are taken, some bad, some good, maybe a few close to perfect. My apprenticeship as an oarsman continues to teach me patience and the understanding that there is no perfection, no end. There is the process, and the striving for consistency. The cosmic balance to all of this seemingly ageless philosophical row/life Zen wisdom is the unwavering truth that in the rest of my life I am just a big kid who wakes up every morning feeling that the world is his playground. Even on the days that seem filled with nothing but manure, I expect to find a pony just around the bend.

In this story, just around the bend is a humbling, life changing adventure exploring the physical and spiritual potential of the aging human body. There is manure, but also lots of ponies; Fear and doubt, pain and fatigue, and the empowerment and enlightenment of letting go.

1. PRINCETON TO PRINCETON

As I begin my descent into New Jersey, my body is confused and agitated. My mind follows. It's been a six-hour flight from Oregon, immobilized with my thoughts and unlimited coffee. My body is accustomed to expending enormous amounts of energy daily. The last week before a big race, the necessary taper in training feels almost cruel. Two days before the race I do absolutely nothing. Now, as I focus on the races ahead of me, I am aching for battle.

Steve drove down to Princeton from New York yesterday. The plan is to meet at Mercer Lake and get in one training row with our new lineup this evening. In rock star fashion, a driver is waiting for me at Newark International Airport's arrivals gate. Tall guy, black coat, white shirt, black tie, holding the card that says Baxter on it, you've seen him before. From Newark I am chauffeured to Princeton. I change into trou (racing shorts) and a T-shirt in the back seat. The time is going to be tight.

I pull up to the roped off entrance at Mercer Lake in the black Lincoln Town Car and Steve is standing right there waiting for me, as if we had planned to meet at that exact spot. He flashes a giant, gaping smile to match his giant frame, eyes wide and sparkling. He is out of breath and drenched in sweat, both from the September humidity and the fact that he has already won his first race in a stroke for stroke battle to the finish. His boat, the Rude and Smooth, edged out Palm Beach Rowing Association by .286 of one second in a six boat final.

There is a one-hour window for training before all boats have to be off the water for the night. The day is going according to plan, but we have to run – first to Steve's rental car to drop my backpack, then to the course. Now we have less than an hour to get on the course in the monster rolodex boat and take a few strokes together before racing tomorrow morning at the highest level of Masters rowing. A rolodex boat is one where you essentially go through your contact list to assemble the best athletes you can, to put together the fastest boat that you can, regardless of where they are from. This practice is often frowned upon in club rowing circles, as it undermines the club philosophy. The club philosophy suggests that athletes in a club be members of the same club and live within a certain radius of that club. I think that most rowers have a love/hate relationship with rolodex crews – we love to hate them until we are invited to be in one, at which point a certain moral and ethical amnesia sets in, and then rolodex crews are positively and without reservation the greatest thing in the world and why doesn't everyone see that? I look across and there, in slings, is the world championship winning eight-oared shell, the Rusty Wailes. This is the boat that we will race. Giants loom.

Rusty was a member of the 1956 Olympic Mens eight. Rowing historian Peter Mallory interviewed him in 2001, "A year before he died while out rowing, Rusty Wailes looked back, "Anything worthwhile in life, you pay for in advance—anything that is not worthwhile you can get in the twinkling of an eye," Wailes wrote. "I have often been asked whether winning a gold medal was worth it. I have replied, 'I learned more about myself and my fellow men in six minutes of rowing than I did in four years at college."

Giants come in all shapes and sizes. In the realm of the coxswain, the on-water coach and leader, the biggest giant of my era is Peter Cipollone, 2004 Olympic gold medalist. Chip will be our coxswain for both events, in charge of, ostensibly, steering. What makes him an Olympian, though, is his ability to cultivate a result of human performance that his individual athletes might not otherwise produce by themselves. I introduce myself and tell him what a pleasure it is to be here. He responds, "It will be even more of a pleasure tomorrow when we kick some #$%^&* ass, 'cause that's how we roll around here." Indeed.

Rigging is checked, footstretchers adjusted (rigging and footstretchers are integral parts of the boat; More on that later). There is little time for introductions. "Hands on the eight!" Chip barks. Giants move. Dave Potter will be in the stroke seat followed by Brian Jamieson, Steve, me, Joe Michels, Eric Stevens, Jim Millar and Rick Smith. The deep blue hull bears the markings USA and Polaroid, the official sponsor of the U.S. National Team. Eric was supposed to be in five seat, but his hip is giving him trouble. He suggests that I row five and he will row three seat and we'll see how the boat moves.

We push off the dock into quiet water and heavy air. It is humid. Most of these guys have rowed together before. Some have probably pushed one another to the brink of death before. The thought is humbling. I have rowed with Dave, Eric and Steve in a 4+, medaling at Boston's Head of the Charles, so I am not completely alien in this boat. But I definitely get the impression that Olympic silver medalist Jamieson suspects me unworthy, an unknown with no national team experience. During the warm-up, hell, during the entire flight over, I, too, have questioned my worthiness. It is human nature to experience self-doubt in the face of great challenge. But I know that what matters is that I have trained and peaked properly over the last 40 weeks, so there can be no excuses. Just pull hard. Crush and kill. Chip takes us through an easy warm-up to get everybody dialed in, and then we work on some starts and some power pieces. There is an astounding amount of power in this boat. It is intoxicating to be a part of this, to be contributing to it.

The pressure is intense. When I think too much I get in my own way. I start to think too much. I'm in New Jersey, home to the United States National Team, rowing in a world championship boat, rowing with some of my heroes.

"Andy, come out clean."

Oh. Shit. I am thinking too much, tightening up, getting stuck at the finish. Cipollone, savage competitor, fearless leader of men, is calm and assured.

"Hands away at the same speed they come in. Let the oar take you with it, one continuous motion, nice and clean."

Chip is relaxed and smiling, "OK, boys, let's take it in."

The 2006 FISA World Rowing Masters Regatta in Princeton, New Jersey, is my biggest rowing adventure to date. More than 7,000 of the best rowers from 45 countries around the world gather for this event. Steve and I have trained hard with one goal in mind, to do well here. This annual event could have been held anywhere - Amsterdam, Budapest, Heidelberg, Prague, Lithuania. For it to land on our East Coast was like having it in our own backyard. And to be in Princeton, home of the U.S. Olympic Training Center, seemed to be a sign of sorts, a cosmic nudge in the right direction. The cost and complexity of getting to a big regatta in another country can be prohibitive. This was a stroke of luck.

We rowed well all last season, even rowing down from our age level and beating some of the younger guys. The idea was to keep going up to higher levels of competition, to see how far this story would take us. We had half-kidded each other that if we did well at World's we should see if we could get ourselves a spot on the 2008 Olympic team. Although it began as an off-handed joke, it took on a life of its own. Now it's already been decided. If we do well we will set a new goal – to take our training to a new level, an Olympic level of commitment, focus, sacrifice, pain, fear, and self-examination. Here at Worlds, Steve and I will be rowing together in a C4+ and a C8+ (a four-man boat and an eight-man boat with coxswain). Age groups delineate masters rowing events. The "A" category represents an average age of those in the boat between 27 and 35. The "B" category is 36 to 42, "C" is 43 to 49, and "D" is 50 to 54, and so on. If we get crushed, we will not be returning to Princeton in 2008 for the Olympic Trials.

I don't remember sleeping that night. I don't remember not sleeping either. I don't remember putting the Rusty Wailes on the water. But I do remember the lineup.

"So what do you think," I asked Eric, "do you want me to take three seat?" His reply was swift – "No, stay in five, this lineup feels good."

For some, the glory seats in an eight-man boat are eight seat (stroke seat) and seven seat. The stroke sets the rate and leads the crew. Seven seat is his bodyguard, protecting him from the other twelve hundred pounds of oarsmen slamming sternward. Oarsmen on the port side tend to follow the stroke and those on starboard side tend to follow seven seat. For me, the glory seats are in the *engine room*, the middle seats. This is where the strongest guys get to just crank on it. I am about to go to the line smack dab in the middle of the engine room, five seat. I will prove to Eric that his decision is sound. I will not let him down.

I am not overly nervous at the start. I am part of a greater, seemingly invincible whole. We cannot lose. Chip does not give us that option. He tells us what we are going to do and how we are going to do it. All I have to do is sacrifice my body, do exactly what Chip tells me to do and be willing to die in that effort. That is a liberating reality for me: simple, deliberate and final. As we sit ready at the starting line at 9:04 a.m., mere seconds from the sounding of the horn and the red light giving way to the green, I think that to be a perfectly acceptable, even comforting plan.

Everything is very quiet, almost peaceful. And then everything is not. The violence that ensues reminds me of the gritty film technique used in the battle scenes in *Saving Private Ryan*. There is shouting and splashing water and strong, well trained warriors applying superhuman, terrible amounts of power to crush their opponents in a violent ballet of physical performance – part symphony of movement, part crocodilian death roll.

I try to keep my head forward by looking over Steve's shoulder and focusing on Brian's. Brian's shoulder and Cipollone's voice become my universe. Insulated in that manner, it seems I forget to breathe. I have never been in an eight-man boat like this before. We cross the 500-meter mark in 1:28.375, less a mark than an afterthought. At 800 meters I am coming out of my trance, just getting the sense that I am breathing hard, just starting to acknowledge the ringing in my ears. Why am I coming out of my zone? I feel like the anesthesia is wearing off before the surgery is over. What is going on? I look out over the course to see that we have opened up the entire field. The closest boat is six seconds back. That is the *closest* boat in a six lane event. Chip is talking us down, lengthening us out. We still work hard, of course, just not life or death hard. We swing through those last 200 meters, crossing the finish line in 3:00.724. At this event there is no silver or bronze medal, only gold. It is an amazing feeling. I don't want it to end. We have the privilege of rowing directly to the medals dock. I can hardly believe that I'm here, now, part of this spectacular effort, after leaving my home in Ashland, Oregon only yesterday.

But there is still the Men's C4+ event coming up. This feels like the warm-up. There is more in the tank. I am so amped from the win that I border on giddy. I duck out of the sun and guzzle my crazy concoction of Cytosport products - Cytomax, Fast Twitch and Muscle Energy. They're working.

FISA, the International Rowing Federation and governing body for international rowing, uses the "static refereeing" system, so it is very quiet at the start with no launches running outboard motors. This second race at 1:05 p.m. is a battle in a four-man boat. We are loose and now we are also extremely confident. The light turns green and we go off the line as if we are launched off an aircraft carrier, immediately taking a deck length. Loose and confident coming off of a big win, it turns out, is a very positive combination.

Loud enough for our opponents to hear, Chip roars "Five strokes in and I've got nothing but bow balls. Let's lose these %^&*#*'s now. They're not worthy!"

We are pistons, impervious to pain, thermal breakdown, bullets, whatever - unstoppable, undeniable. This is the Bulldog lineup, Steve's Yale crewmates, with whom we rowed so well in Boston – Dave Potter at stroke seat, me at three, Steve at two and Eric at bow seat. Typically your bow seat is your smallest guy. Eric is 6'6".

The start is as close to perfect as rowing can get – power, fluidity, synchronicity. One might hope to simply hang on to the space gained in those first five strokes and that would be enough, but not for us. Not today. Today we would take more. There are different parts of a race with applications for power, for length, and for sprinting. In this particular race with these particular guys we just continue to build, and build, and build. Crushing, savage, primal, it seems the boat, a Hudson shell, might break all the way to the end. As far as I can tell we are still accelerating when we cross the finish line. We win by 8.882

seconds in a seven-lane field, answering my doubts a second time, *I am worthy.*

Afterward, standing around the boat slings, Chip and Brian are laughing, Gold medals hanging from their necks. The suspicion is gone from Brian's face, a bright smile in its place. The two Olympians shake hands and Brian says, "Any time, any place."

Later in the day we make our way to the beer garden at the finish line. My gold medals clank against my chest, an audible reminder of what we have just accomplished. I catch Steve's look and understand that my noisy accessories are unseemly, like bragging. Sheepishly I take off the medals, curbing my jubilation only barely.

Steve has now won three Gold medals at the highest level of Masters rowing, and I have won two. There is no getting around the fact that this is a pretty big deal. I am happy that my 40-week training plan for us has paid off so well. I am also happy that I held my own with the giants. I am a pup as compared to the curriculum vitae of my boat mates.

In the beer garden, after many celebratory Guinness's, Jim Millar, teammate of Steve's at Yale and informal patriarch of the Princeton Training Center, says, "Look at this kid. He hops on a plane from Oregon, comes over here and walks away with two Gold medals in one day. Not a bad gig when you can get it, huh Baxter?"

We collapse into white folding chairs near the finish line at the base of the three-story viewing tower. On this side of the lake are all participants, spectators, cars, and boat trailers for this worldwide event. All boats launch from this side and return to this side, like bees from and to the hive. On the opposite side of Mercer Lake in ominous view sits the embodiment of elite rowing; a six boat bay castle – the Finn Caspersen Olympic Training Center. It is September 2006. In April 2008, nineteen months from now, Steve and I will launch on to this same body of water – from the opposite side of the lake, and a world away.

2. THE SET

I moved to Ashland, Oregon in late 2000. I had been running my gym, New Angle Fitness, in the Rockridge district of Oakland and rowing for Lake Merritt Rowing Club at that time. As a Medical Exercise Specialist and Post Rehabilitation Conditioning Specialist dealing predominantly in load-bearing joints and joint replacements, my clientele just naturally formatted itself to the over fifty demographic. This became my niche in the highly competitive San Francisco Bay Area fitness arena. After a successful consulting job designing a gym for Mountain Meadows Retirement Community in Ashland, Oregon, I would become their Director of Health and Fitness. The dot.com explosion was in full swing at that time, and life in the Bay Area was becoming increasingly unrealistic for a small business owner with a young family. I wondered if Ashland had rowing.

While attending the USRowing conference in December of 2000, Chris Ives and I were talking about the possibility of a rolodex boat for the San Diego Crew Classic in April of 2001. Chris is a former National Team rower and present day indoor rowing guru.

I told Chris that I was moving to Ashland, Oregon. He casually mentioned that Steve Kiesling lived in Ashland. I was flattered and excited; flattered that Ives would want me in a boat with him and excited at the prospect of meeting Kiesling. How would I initiate that? Would I contact his press agent, or write a formal letter, or pass a series of grueling physical tests to prove that I am worthy of his audience? Chris, eating a banana, suggested, "Might try the phone book."

When I got home I called information and easily got Steve's number. Apparently a formal letter wasn't necessary. He answered his phone. I introduced myself, explained the recent chain of events in the fast yet halted speech pattern that I often exhibit when I'm nervous, and awaited a response. He was coaching a high school girls rowing team, created serendipitously, the brainchild of a student named Jennifer Traynor. Now he was going to move on to start a college program at Southern Oregon University. The high school had a replacement coach lined up but needed an assistant coach. I asked if he might be willing to meet for lunch and show me the program. Again I awaited a response. Three hundred and fifty miles later I pulled in to Emigrant Lake to meet the author of *The Shell Game*.

My first impression of Steve was the obvious - Steve is big. My second impression was that he is aloof. Reticent to make eye contact, he seems to be always thinking three things, but talking about half of one thing. Of course, we had just met for the first time, and what did I know about this guy? No more than he knew about me, I suppose. We ate some deli sandwiches on the tailgate of his truck. In the back of the truck were a gas can and an outboard motor. Sandwiches devoured, we got in so he could show me around.

I was excited to see their facility. We drove along the lake past the park entrance. The Emigrant Lake Park has a big water slide, actually two water slides side by side. One climbs a flight of stairs to the top of the water slide and then goes down the water slide, and then repeats the process, stopping only to refuel with requisite hotdog and ice cream bar fare. In the bushes, underneath the water slide and its wrought iron skeleton, survives a beat up old eight person rowing shell. Next to that is Steve's own single scull. That is the program, two boats.

One boat, really. Steve's single doesn't count. No boathouse. In fairness, why would you want a whole boathouse for just one boat? That would be silly. No dock. No path to the lake. Well, there's that outboard motor and that nifty gas can. Presumably, somewhere in the bushes, there is a dingy, a coach's launch, that attaches to the outboard. Or I could just stand on the shore and shout as the boats, the one boat, goes by, sitting on my outboard and waving my gas can. Things can only go up from here. What's that? No pay, you say? Where do I sign up? Pay would ruin this whole picture. Money would taint the purity of this scene. Yes, that is what I will tell my wife, Denise, when I get home, I thought. Surely she will understand that we are staring at a rare opportunity, a diamond in the rough!

The diamond in the rough metaphor could not have been truer. It was Steve's diamond. Underneath that water slide, unpolished and as yet unrealized, lay the genesis of the Ashland Rowing Club.

I drove home. Denise asked, "What's Steve like?" I answered, "Steve is big…and he is aloof." House sold, moving truck packed, we loaded up our two great Danes, two-year-old son Garrett, and headed north.

So began my friendship with Steve Kiesling and our pursuit of all things stupid. If a particular idea seemed improbable, against the grain, or foolish, that was all the incentive we needed. If one of us did anything individually stupid, we would call the other to revel in the stupidity. He told me how he crashed a Jaguar. I told him about how I wrestled a grizzly bear. Once, in January, I charged down the dock with faithful dog and loving son at my side, diving headlong into the snow melted waters of Emigrant Lake. My faithful dog and loving son stopped short, proving what many already knew - I am stupider than my dog.

One time Steve called with the announcement, "I pulled a tree out of the ground." We both have property and both share horror stories about weekend chores. I replied with the affirmation that a tractor is invaluable because you can just throw a chain around the base of the tree and – "No, I mean *I pulled a tree out of the ground. It wasn't easy. I think I might pay for that tomorrow.*" You get the idea.

We drove to regattas together, as little as three hours drive to as much as two days, swapping stories and histories. When the distance was greater than that, we flew. We got to know each other beyond the framework of rowing, although rowing is what brought us together. As the years rowed by, we had amassed new stories, our own stories. In the last eight years, Steve has been a hero; mentor, brother, supporter, collaborator and friend, often times in combination. Not that it has always been smooth, but it has never been dull and the fun quotient has always been extremely high.

Steve and I started rowing the Pair in preparation for the U.S. Masters National Championships in Sacramento, California in 2003. Prior to that we were rowing in fours and eights. At some point Steve said, "We should row a Pair." That sounds exciting and utterly terrifying so I say, "Really?" Steve is casual, "Sure. It'll either suck or it won't. We'll find out pretty quick." Since we're both big guys with a lot of experience, both ports (we pull a single oar that enters the water on the left-hand side of the boat), and neither one of us is too bright, we thought this was a splendid idea. I spent a few months learning to row starboard (pulling a single oar that enters the water on the right side of the boat) and we trained in a fairly beat up but much loved shell made by Hudson Boat Works. After a tune up at the Northwest Regional Championships in Vancouver, Washington, we lurched our way down the course for a bronze medal at the U.S. Masters National Championships. I don't remember the margin of victory, but when we crossed the line I was reasonably sure that first place finishers Berkeley Johnson and Craig Webster had already showered and dressed and were working on their second margaritas.

In 2004 we won a gold medal in the men's pair in a seven-lane final at the Canadian Masters National Championships in Victoria, British Columbia. In 2005 we got a wild idea – to race our Pair in the A category at the Masters World Games in Edmonton, Canada. Steve and I are a C pair. To go to a World Master's event and race down two age categories against the likes of Australia, Russia, Italy, Canada, and other heavy hitters is no small thing. It's preposterous. In fact it's so preposterous that I don't remember even being nervous. If we got creamed, so what? What did we have to lose? After making it through heats, we finished fourth in the A final. I don't speak Russian, but based on universal perceptions of intonation and inflection, Russian rowers who lose to old American rowers swear a lot. Standing at the results board afterward, most eyes were turned upward at the numbers being posted. But two sets of eyes kept looking at Steve and me. I recognized that this pair had been in our race. They were Americans. I was about to extend my hand and thank them for a great race, but before I could do this one of them blurted, "How *old are* you guys?" We had beaten them in the final.

In 2006 we put together a more structured training regimen, with serious attention paid to our strength program, and shook hands on an idea that heretofore had been kicked around only in an unceremonious way: If we did well at the FISA Masters World Championships in Princeton, we decided, we would train for the Olympic trials in 2008.[1]

---

[1] FISA is the French acronym for Federation Internationale des Societes d'Aviron. In English that is the International Federation of Rowing Associations (Abbreviated that is the Int Fed of Row Ass's).

To row the pair is to row with a giant microscope above you at all times. If you don't row well in the pair, there are only two people to blame. If the boat's not going straight at full pressure, someone's getting pulled around or the catch timing is off. If your partner is an Olympian, it's probably you. If you pretend it's not you and start looking around for the third rower who is screwing things up, then you flip. We were now about to embark on a journey that would ultimately find us rowing right under one of the biggest microscopes in the rowing world – the 2008 Olympic Trials.

Rowing has many idiosyncrasies, not the least of which is you face backward, sternward to propel the shell, or scull, forward. A Pair (2-) is a sweep boat that has two athletes with one oar per athlete. A "Pair with" (2+) has two athletes plus a coxswain, who steers the boat. This particular boat is called "the lead (pronounced led) sled," as the power to weight ratio of having to drag that extra human around is nothing short of sadistic. Other sweep boats are the straight four with no coxswain (4-), the four with coxswain (4+), and the eight with coxswain (8+). Orientation and language are based on the vessel facing forward, even though the athlete is facing backward. Steve rows port and I row starboard in our Pair configuration. This means that Steve's oar is on the left side of the boat and my oar is on the right side of the boat, even though from our perspective it is just the opposite. Sculling boats have two oars per athlete. Examples of sculling boats are the double (2x) and the quad (4x). Traditionalists call two-oared rowing sculling and one-oared sweep rowing, well, rowing. I have always taken some comfort in the distinction. As a collegiate sweep rower, trained and ingrained, I see sculling as somehow strange, evil and wrong. By the time of the Olympic trials I would be 41 and Steve would be 49. Was this a realistic goal? Were we crazy, just plain stupid or both? Could we possibly hold our own in the Pair, the most difficult boat in rowing? Between the two of us we won five gold medals in Princeton that weekend. So, as agreed, we were going to find out. As Steve would say, "This promises to be a grand adventure!"

3. THE VIOLENT BALLET

The path that Stephen Kiesling followed to get to the starting point of this story is certainly more grandiose than my own. He followed his sister, Jenny, to Yale. Both rowed. Steve excelled at it, rowing through the ranks at Yale, making the U.S. National team and then the Olympic team. That was 1980; the year the United States boycotted the Olympics. He never got to compete: He wrote a book about his experiences, entitled *The Shell Game*. In the world of rowing it is a classic. It was a *New York Times* best seller, although the powers that be at Yale deemed it worthy only of a B grade.

After 1980, Steve moved to Ireland for a few years before returning to start training in earnest for the 1984 pair trials with Matthew Labine. They had a brilliant heat, "as close to God" as one could come while rowing a boat. The final, unfortunately, was not to be as transcendent.

Realizing that his elite rowing career was winding down, he was setting his sights on getting a real job when he met his mentor, former *Psychology Today* editor and author T. George Harris. In association with T. George, Steve would spend the next six years at *American Health* magazine. He also spearheaded Nike's *Cross-Training* program and freelanced for *Sports Illustrated* and the *New Yorker,* among others. Much of the nineties were spent chasing corporate pirates for his book, *Walking the Plank*. Then came two beautiful children, Tim and Alexandria. In 1998, *Spirituality & Health* magazine hit the stands. Now, ten years later, Steve is the Editor-in-Chief.

I rowed at Humboldt State University, California in the early nineties. We were a small program with heart and the kind of enthusiasm that belies a bunch of athletic misfits with nothing to lose. We trained, with ferocity and intent, under our coach Jeff Strayer. Jeff had rowed at Orange Coast College, a two year program where they were known as The Giant Killers for their heroic efforts against much larger programs. We likened ourselves Giant Killers.

The emotions of rowing - the fears, the joys, the kinesthetic memories, the commitments and the sacrifices - all rowers, novice and Olympian alike, share these. One may be relatively faster than the other, but the battles being fought, internally and externally, are no less real for either.

Row Diary 4/19/07:

I spoke last week with Ed McNeely, exercise physiologist for RowCanada, about training for the Olympic trials one year from now. Ed thought this challenge was a good idea as long as we paid special attention to diet as it relates to recovery and preservation of muscle mass. This morning I spoke with Dr. Fritz Hagerman, exercise physiologist at Ohio University and for the U.S. National Rowing Team. Fritz echoed our motto – train smart; quality over quantity (our other motto is "Out of my way, Sonny," but more on that later). At our age we are experienced enough to know when the volume of work is exceeding our ability to recover from it. In 2006 I put together a 40-week training program for us leading up to the FISA Masters World Championships. After the first month of that program we both realized that we could not handle the volume of work. Rather than follow that regimen to the letter, we would adjust the volume intuitively. This was smart.

The notion of my making the Olympic team was fanciful at best, but I really thought Steve could do it. My idea was that I would serve as a coach/trainer/pair partner for Steve up to the point where he would need a stronger athlete in order to move forward. When I spoke with USRowing about the trials, I explained this to them, and they said that they could facilitate providing a candidate to maximize Steve's chances. Secretly I had hoped that I might make it all the way to the end with Steve, but this was the official plan so I was prepared to be cast aside at the appropriate time. I told Fritz that my erg scores (Concept 2 ergometer, or "erg" for short. These are rowing machines, just like the ones you would find at your local gym) could not match Steve's, but that our relative strength was practically identical, and that our boat went straight and usually crossed the finish line before anybody else's boat did. Fritz disagreed with the idea of bringing in a substitute in a refreshingly forceful and confident manner, "You've just answered your own question. If we pull a senior out of the University of Washington varsity eight and put him in your place a month before the trials it will just upset the boat!" The flaw in this perspective is that relative strength - the theoretical mathematical calculation of boat speed based on power relative to body weight - is just numbers on paper. What can't be calculated, what can't be quantified is the savagery of the Olympian.

Row Diary 4/24/07:

The good news is I think we can beat Argentina, India, and probably Egypt. To date our best 1,000-meter time in the pair is 3:33. Doubling that time and adding 8 to 10 seconds would give a rough estimate of what to expect over a 2,000 meter course at our current conditioning and experience; something around 7:14–7:16. In the 2000 Olympics Egypt pulled a 7:15.63 in the heat. India pulled 7:16.10. In the 2004

Olympics the Australian men's pair of James Tomkins and Drew Ginn won gold with a 6:30. Argentina, at the same Olympics, 7:19. So at the very least, we wouldn't get laughed at publicly. I believe it to be bad form to laugh at old people publicly, and I would not want to be so inconsiderate as to put someone in that uncomfortable position.

I have never been a *great* rower. In college I was probably U.S. development camp fodder, not worthy of the U.S. national team. For every Stephen Kiesling there are probably forty or so Andy Baxter's. Bryan Volpenhein is one of our country's current rowing superstars, and for good reason. For every Bryan Volpenhein there are probably ten Steve Kieslings. So if Steve, former Olympic team member, legend and icon is in over his head in his Olympic quest, than mine must be positively quixotic. Steve talks about telling stories – the stories we tell others and the stories we tell ourselves. He has choices. He could go back to Philadelphia and train at Penn AC with his former coach, Ted Nash. He could go to the National Team camp. He could train with Steve Kominsky, former junior national champion currently pulling national team caliber ergometer scores. Any of these options would make a great story, so why would he choose to train and compete with me? What's my story? How do I justify being here?

More than likely I am a convenience on many levels. I have two gyms in the Southern Oregon valley, so training is convenient. Logistically I am a convenience as I can build the considerable training volume into my work; we are friends and travel well together, have a similar sense of humor and philosophical outlook on life. Also I am probably as close a partner in fitness and age to Steve as he is going to find in a 50-mile radius who also happens to know how to row. So I guess that all of those factors in sum would make me a pretty good partner after all. And, as Steve says, I am up for the adventure. That is no small thing. Showing up is no small thing.

We decided to put together a fourteen-month training plan leading up to the trials. Along the way we would have benchmarks consisting of ergometer tests and specific races. These races would be, in chronological order:

6/22/07 - the US Rowing Masters' Northwest Regional Championships, Vancouver, Washington. We will race the B pair, the C pair, the C four and the D eight.

8/17/07 - the Canadian Masters' National Championships, Victoria, British Columbia. We will race the AA-C pair, C four, D four, mixed C eight and the D eight.

10/20/07 - Head of the Charles regatta, Boston, Massachusetts. We will race the Master's four event.

3/10/08 - Lake Natoma, California. We will compete in a series of pair races against the Sacramento State University Men's Crew.

4/5/08 - the San Diego Crew Classic, Mission Bay, California. We will race the Club eight event.

4/25/08 - the US Olympic Trials, Finn Casperson Olympic Training Center, Princeton, New Jersey.

I spent all of yesterday mapping out the first macrocycle of our training plan. This is the seventeen-week period from now until the Canadian Masters National Championships, August 17.

Designing a training plan is an art form integrating science with experience and intuitive guesswork. Like rowing itself, a lot of where you want to go depends on where you have been. The Northwest Championships would be a tune-up along the way. Within that period are microcycles, phases that focus on different energy systems and their physiological adaptations — the preparatory phase, the pre-competitive phase, the taper, and the competitive phase. These phases focus primarily on the energy systems as they relate to the mechanical patterns of the given sport, in this case rowing. For the most part, fitness improvements need to be sport specific. I love to mountain bike, and live in one of the greatest places in the world for doing it. No one would deny that mountain biking is great exercise. But for an athlete the principle of sport specificity dictates that the best way to "get better" at something is to practice that specific movement, in our case on the water or on a Concept 2 rowing ergometer. Cycling will make your legs stronger, but the adaptation will not have the same neuromuscular pattern as the leg drive in the rowing stroke. Wind sprints at the track are great for your cardiopulmonary system, but will not translate well to rowing as the two activities recruit and enhance different proportions of fast and slow twitch muscle fibers; different speed, different mechanics, different load, different dynamics of power, and so forth.

Contained within this macrocycle is another set of microcycles devoted to weight training. These are the symmetry/hypertrophy phase, the maximum strength phase, the power phase, and the power-endurance phase. Increases in strength and power will ultimately be measured in Relative Strength (strength relative to body weight). In fact, the phrase *pulling your own weight* originates from rowing. The Oxford English Dictionary defines pulling your own weight, "to row with effect in proportion to one's weight." The general idea of a training macrocycle is to gradually increase both the volume and intensity of work up to a point just prior to an important competition. At that point one decreases the volume of work, but not the intensity or the number of sessions. This is the taper. During the taper your body "super-compensates," placing you and your pair partner ready at the starting line with the smoldering intensity of the twin oarsmen of the apocalypse.

Row Diary 4/27/07:

5:30 a.m. back in the pair for the first time since the August 2006 U.S. Masters National Championships in Seattle, Washington. Since that time, burned out on the pair, we have been in fours and eights. Terrible row in Seattle: tight, jacked up, no length, no ratio, no focus, blah, blah, blah. We won a silver medal and I was disappointed. Had I never rowed a pair again that would have been just fine. Stick with fours and eights. Sit down in the engine room, shut up and row. The engine room is the middle of the boat and typically where you would put your stronger athletes. Not as technically demanding as the stroke seat or the bow seat, the engine room generates power forward with less potential to "push" or "pinch" the boat to one side or another.

One possible explanation for our silver medal that August only now occurs to me. I had broken my back in July. I was unloading hay bales out of my truck, bending, twisting, then accelerating, twisting and throwing. Pop. An MRI revealed a vertical disk herniation through the endplate of the L5 vertebrae, technically a broken back. It hurt. I was less than a week from leaving for a two-week family vacation in Spain at my father-in-law's villa in Moraira. That was going to require drugs. Now with the broken back maybe I could get some. That's a joke. Actually the drugs were to get me through the twenty-one hours spent on airplanes and in airports. Below is an entry from that time.

Back Shot –

October 16, 2006 was my last workout. Monday morning I rowed a 5k on the erg, and then in the afternoon 7860 meters. And that was it. I was done. Five weeks after winning two gold medals at FISA master worlds, I gave in to the pain of a broken back. Two weeks of physical *therapy and massage therapy had begun to strip away the muscular splinting that enabled me to accomplish that feat. I had to change my reality to accomplish that. This was a new reality. As the muscles began to let go, they exposed me not as the world champion of five weeks ago. They exposed a harsh new reality that I was broken. Some days I couldn't drive a car without crying from the pain. I had diarrhea from the inflammation in my back literally cooking my bowels. Boy, that's not even fun to read about, much less feel. But here is the kicker. As bad as the next six weeks would be physically, they simply could not hold a candle to the emotional stress of being disconnected from my self. Rowing is a big part of who I am. My ability to express myself through physicality, specifically rowing, is a part of the definition of me. Having that taken away is a form of trauma, an amputation, a different kind of train wreck. I don't like being helped, and I could barely, and I do mean barely, tie my own shoes. I would break out in fever sweats trying to put my pants on. All in all, the daily ritual of getting out of bed and going through the obligatory steps to start the day, just like everyone else on the planet, was gruesome. And none of that hurt as much as looking down at my training calendar, the documentation of my existence, and seeing those two words, **back shot,** staring back at me.*

In the small coastal town of Moraira, Spain I found Euro Gym's version of a rowing machine a great, hulking beast with footstretchers welded to the side of the frame at almost seat height and some form of an electric brake. The readout had flashing lights that lit up vertically to represent a resistance of one to ten. Numbers one through eight felt like a split of 2:30 (a split tells you in minutes and seconds how long it would take to row 500 meters), damper #1 at 25 strokes per minute on a Concept 2 ergometer; in layman's terms, practically no resistance. So, of course, nine felt like a split of, oh, maybe pulling a friggin' microbus out of the Mediterranean...

damper #10 … at 8 spm - Heavy. But this is the only gym within walking distance and I didn't have access to a car, courtesy of whoever it is in Madrid who now had my driver's license.

Nothing can prepare one for the humidity and heat of Costa Blanca in July. Beer is served half a glass at a time; a full glass would be warm before you could finish it. The culture revolves around the heat. The gym opens at 10 a.m. because dinner is at 10 p.m. when things cool down. The gym then closes at 1 p.m. while everyone sleeps through the hottest part of the day, reopening its doors at 4 p.m. There is no air conditioning and the view of the ocean from Euro Gym's windows is so stunning there are no shades on them – heat, humidity, still air and direct sunlight. I winced at the thought of even bending down to get on to the rowing seat, white hot pain shooting down my back. This was going to be a character builder.

I wouldn't say that I was sweating during my erg workouts. I would say that I was expressing water with such force and in such prolific volume that my clothing was nothing more than a filter for snaring salt. If salt was still a commodity I could have paid for my criminally high gym membership fee with my t-shirt.

Steve and I were fully committed to our training program for the FISA Masters World Championships. Broken back or not, this was our biggest adventure to date and I was not going to miss it. Surviving the Mediterranean microbus was enough of a test to assure me I should continue. The Seattle Masters National Championship was not meant to be our peak, but the primer leading up to Worlds. At the time I was crushed by that Silver, but now I see that it was a perfect fit to a larger puzzle. The back issue may have been just the break I needed *not* to peak at Nationals.

Row Diary 4/30/07:

Second day back in the pair on a gorgeous Sunday morning. We start with pause drills then two steady state pieces at a low 20 strokes per minute (ultimately we will race at 36 spm). Pause drills are technical exercises during which you pause at specific points in the rowing stroke to help with balance, control, and body position (relative to each other). Kinesthetic awareness, the brain's ability to know what the body is doing in time and space, is extremely important in rowing, especially in the pair. First, there is the obvious; these boats are tiny and rowers are big. You have a shell that weighs a bit over 58 pounds and you are going to put two athletes with a total body weight of about 420 pounds smack dab in the middle of it. Second, and less obvious to the layperson, there are only two oars, one per person; one brain controlling his body and his oar in time and space, another brain controlling his. Imagine having two brains. One brain controls the left leg and the other brain controls the right leg independently. Try to walk. Try to jog. Try to sprint with power and control and in a straight line. Now do it backwards. This is the violent ballet of rowing.

Steve suggests that we take some video of us and send it to his former coach, Tony Johnson. Tony knows a thing or two about pairs (Olympic Silver and two time World champion with partner Larry Hough). If we continue to surround ourselves with such great people, we might actually start to look like we know what we're doing.

I have always told my clients that some of the greatest workouts are the ones where you don't really want to show up. A morning in early May was just such an occasion. 5:30 a.m. at the boathouse and it was starting to rain and I was in a T-shirt and we just got the new speed coach and I would rather install the wiring for it and do a steady state on the erg and I don't have a hat and I think I have a paper cut and what's that, Lassie? Miner's trapped in a cave and …

and we go out and have one of the greatest rows ever — *ever*. So much of the row-life parallel is showing up. Nothing ventured, nothing gained and all that. After all, that is the fundamental philosophy of our quest – to show up. Then, once you show up, *get out of your own way*. This is essential in rowing, as in life. So many of our limitations are self imposed.

At the 2005 World Rowing Masters games in Edmonton we were fourth in the A pair final and I was ecstatic. Not even a medal to show for it, yet one of my proudest moments. Why? Because we showed up. We set a goal, outlined a plan of how to get to that goal, and trained toward that goal. After you achieve optimum fitness and technical proficiency, you work on your race plan. You train and rehearse your race plan both mentally and physically until it is burned into your muscle memory. You have now done everything within your control to prepare. If you race with singular intent and focus, execute your race plan and cross the line with an empty tank, then you have won! It doesn't matter whether another boat finished in front of you, because you have rowed the very best race that you could row. You can't control what you can't control, so why throw energy at it? Of course there may be times when you have to adapt to outside influences, but the principle is just the same. How you respond to that adversity is as much a mark of your character and your will along the path to your reaching for your goal as anything else. This is the religion and the philosophy. This is the row-life parallel.

Within the rowing stroke are phases. When the oar blade is in the water you are applying pressure. This is called the drive. When the oar blade is out of the water, on its way toward the next stroke, this is called the recovery. As a coach, I like to tell my athletes to "disappear" on the recovery. You do your job, then get out of the way and let the boat do its job.

Row Diary 5/2/07:

Spoke with Fritz at length this morning to review the training plan. What a role model. If I can be as passionate about life at 40 as he is at 72 *that* would be Olympic. In addition to his formidable resume in the fields of exercise science, sports performance and physiology, Fritz was himself a master's national champion marathoner in his 40's. He and his wife Marge still maintain vigorous training regimens.

He quoted Ohio State football coach Woody Hayes, "You've got three things going for you, and 2 of 'em are bad." He elaborated, "First, there's the age thing. But second, you're rowing the pair, for Christ sakes!" So our saving grace then, our stroke of genius, is our experience and time together on the water. We are going to take the notion that our mechanical efficiency and neuromuscular patterning, in concert with our optimum relative fitness and training program, will match up to our significantly younger counterparts. One of the reasons that Fritz, acknowledged as one of the world's premiere exercise physiologists and without peer in the rowing world, has agreed to give us the time of day is that we are (more importantly, Steve is) trying to do something that has never been done before. Fritz still has data on Steve from the 1980 Olympic team and had retested him at the Head of the Charles in 2003 as part of a study on elite athlete fitness relative to aging, so I am sure our endeavor piques his interest on a scientific level.

As I say goodbye the esteemed Dr. Hagerman says, "Tell Kiesling that if he doesn't call me I'm gonna take him out in the parking lot and kick his ass in front of all of his friends." Believing this to be a statement of fact, I relay the message to Steve immediately.

Row Diary 5/3/07:

Blood pressure 123/82, Pulse 44 beats per minute. Heart rate and blood pressure, taken regularly, serve as indicators of sufficient recovery and harbingers of overtraining and sickness. If my morning heart rate is over 50 beats per minute, I take care not to over-train or catch a cold. If my blood pressure is greater than 135/85, I breathe deeply, think calming thoughts, and remind myself that the four food groups are not bacon, pizza, Fritos and beer.

Category 6 training sessions, especially on the erg, are what we call slogs. Our energy systems are defined by category – 6 being the lowest intensity and 2 being the highest. There is no 1. Possibly someone will make a mockumentary about rowing a la the movie "Spinal Tap" and then we will have a 1. A slog is a low-intensity piece where we keep heart rate below 140 beats per minute. Typically a slog is also associated with excessively long duration, 60, 80 minutes at a time for instance. The inherent conflict for us with the traditional slog is that it runs counter to our Train Smart philosophy. As older athletes, our focus is on the quality of the work, not the quantity. Says Fritz, "We have convincing data, including muscle biopsy, histochemical and biochemical indicators, which support that rowing continuously at a low, steady-state intensity for 60 minutes or longer for any caliber rower is not more effective in maintaining aerobic capacity than 30 minutes of rowing at the same work intensity." So the key, then, is to be specific in our training as to the energy system utilized in a given session.

Row Diary 5/6/07:

Tried unsuccessfully to install our brand new SpeedCoach performance monitor on the pair the other night. The SpeedCoach will give us valuable data, including our rating in strokes per minute, our meters traveled, and our split, that is, the time to travel 500 meters in minutes and seconds. The split ultimately tells you how much power you are putting out: The lower the number, the greater the power. For instance, if we pull a 1:45/500 split for 1000 meters, we will cover that distance in 3 minutes and 30 seconds. If we pull a 1:44/500 split, we would cross the finish line in 3:28. Turns out the pair is prewired for a StrokeCoach, which is another animal entirely. A StrokeCoach counts your strokes per minute, doesn't do much else. Just kinda sits there and counts some strokes. 'Bout the size of a fast food hash brown. We call it Counter Intelligence. Counter Intelligence aside, we are rowing well.

Row Diary 5/8/07:

Steve suggests changing the pitch on the oars. Before the 2005 World Masters Games we purchased a specialized new oar called a Fat Smoothie made by Peter and Dick Dreissigacker at Concept 2. This oar has a comparatively large blade surface area and is loaded accordingly. If the oarlock has too much pitch, the over-angled oar blade will not "catch" the water sufficiently at the beginning of the stroke (coincidently called "the catch"). It will also "wash out", rising out of the water prematurely toward the end of the stroke ("the finish"). This morning we change the pitch one degree. It is extremely important that any changes we make to our rigging be done in finite increments and one change at a time. Out on the water the Strokecoach refuses to coach strokes, or do much of anything, for that matter. Steve did, repeatedly, what I would have done if I was within reach, but smacking it did not help; curious.

When justifying brute force in any given situation, my dad would say, "Force is the only idiom it knows." When I was a kid I didn't know what that meant but my dad could say anything with enough confidence and authority that it had to be true. He would also say things like "Hold, ye seven blocks of granite." I didn't know what a "ye" was or how much a block weighed, but I knew with unwavering certainty that if anybody could hold seven blocks of granite, Dad was the guy for the job.

I had grown up around adventurers. My dad was, among many other things, one of the founding fathers of the Stanford Alpine Club and a can-do-anything superhero type of guy. My parents were alpine climbers and scaled peaks around the world, including some notable first ascents. Baxter's Pinnacle in the Teton Range of the Rocky Mountains was named for my father. My brothers and I grew up as part of the Sierra Club "family," scrambling on Berkeley's Indian rock, followed by potluck dinners at the home of David Brower, the environmentalist and founder of many organizations, including the Sierra Club Foundation. Sometimes we were gone for weeks camping in the High Sierras. Mom and Dad led at least a dozen Sierra Club trips around the world, including the 17,000-foot Rwenzori Mountains in Uganda. The highest of the Rwenzoris are, like Mount Kilimanjaro and Mount Kenya, permanently snow-capped. Dad once wrote of Mom, "I was, and remain, profoundly respectful of her strength, courage, and determination. I had a great pride when she led the final icy pitch on the highest peak in the Congo."

Row Diary 5/9/07:

Got the new wiring for the StrokeCoach and had a chance to talk with Dick Dreissigacker about rigging numbers for our beloved Hudson pair. The numbers were sobering. Rowing is all about leverage. In Volker Nolte's book *Rowing Faster*, Canadian National Team coach Mike Spracklen writes, "Oars are both first- and second-class levers. As a first-class lever the rowing pin is the fulcrum and the water is the load. As a second-class lever the submerged blade is the fulcrum and the boat or pin is the load. The stroke can be thought of as the blade moving through the water from beginning to finish or the blade remaining stationary in the water as it levers the boat past." How much "load" is built into the oar has a profound impact on boat speed as it relates to rate, power, and length. Too much load and you will not be able to sustain optimal power output (think driving up a steep hill in fifth gear). Not enough load, and you will not be able to apply power efficiently (think driving 60 miles per hour in first gear). Dick suggested a span (distance from center of the boat to the oarlock pin) of 85.5 centimeters and an inboard oar length of 115.5 centimeters. This is a fairly heavy load. The good news is that these rigging numbers will enable us to throw a ton of power at the blade. The bad news is that to translate that power into boat speed it's going to hurt — a lot (think driving up a steep hill in fifth gear at 60 miles per hour). Speed hurts.

Row Diary 5/10/07:

Per Fritz's suggestion, we took a rest day yesterday in preparation for our first 10,000 test. The 10,000 is an all out piece of considerable duration. "All out" is relative. Intensity is always relative to duration. The split/500 that you can pull for 1,000 meters is greater than what you can pull for 2,000 meters, which is greater than what you can pull for 5,000 meters, etc. So, having never done an all out 10,000 piece before, this was going to be a bit of an experiment. Steve and I met at my Medford gym location at 7:00 a.m. We decided that we didn't want to scare anybody, so we put two ergs in the parking lot, went through the obligatory litany of reasons as to why this was a perfectly terrible idea, then sat down and went to work. Rowing 10,000 meters is a matter of finding the maximum sustainable intensity and stroke rate for the job. This requires ongoing assessment, taking inventory both physically and mentally as to what is left in my tank and what I can handle. As I do this my mind devotes significant effort to sabotaging me, telling me what I don't have left in my tank and what I can't handle. Ultimately, when my battle with my inner demon becomes one of symbolic life and death, I get by with this affirmation – no matter what happens, I will not actually die. All but dead, as Holmes suggests, but no one will be dying on the erg today. That seems sensational, but it's that simple. Once you have accepted that, you might as well get to work.

I had a decent 10k piece but went out too hard in the first 4k, paid the price and fell of the pace a bit in the end. Steve had a strong piece and I think, with a slightly higher stroke rate, it would be even stronger. Tomorrow we will be back on the water to test the new rigging, oar load, and gadgetry. Tomorrow is a new day.

Row Diary 5/11/07:

Gadgets suck. Immediate feedback is a brutal, uncaring reminder of where you sit/stand in the row-life continuum. I hate gadgets. This morning we hooked up with three men's singles and a novice men's quad for a steady-state piece. To review, singles, doubles and quads are sculling boats with two oars per athlete; pairs, fours and eights are sweep boats with one oar per athlete. With our impeller and SpeedCoach in place, rigging and oars newly loaded we set off at 23 to 24 strokes per minute. Initially getting used to the new rig, we walk through a single and the quad. Starting to apply some more pressure, I take my first look over Steve's shoulder at the SpeedCoach. Hmm. On the main body of the lake Steve tells me to check my course, as it appears we are not going straight. I am getting pulled around. This means that I am not matching his power. Double hmm. We round the corner heading up the arm, overtaking another single. With unfounded confidence I say, "Now let's go get Scott," the lone sculler ahead of us. Bringing the rate up two beats into a slight headwind, the SpeedCoach shows 2:08. What? A split of 2:08, even into a headwind in a pair, is slow. I am getting frustrated, so naturally I start attacking the catch, ripping water, getting stuck at the finish, and generally making things worse. On top of that we have not caught Scott yet and we are running out of lake. We are in fifth gear and the hill is getting steeper. I call "weigh enough" (stop) just as our bow catches Scott's stern and we debrief. I am feeling particularly weak and demoralized, due in some part to yesterday's 10,000 and today's new rig. Remembering that boat speed is a combination of power, length and rate, we have clearly not utilized rate.

Gadgets rock! Immediate feedback is a positive, life-affirming reminder of where you sit/stand in the row-life continuum. I love gadgets. We pull around to sync up with the other boats for some race starts. This was not part of our planned workout, but neither was rowing slow and badly. BAM! Right off the bat we are pulling 1:36. That's better. We move on to pyramids, 10 on 10 off, 20 on 20 off, 30 on 30 off then back down. We apply power at will without ever going above 29 strokes per minute. All is well again. The adventure will continue.

Row Diary 5/13/07:

Today is mixed. We are moving the boat, but I am still getting stuck at the finish and fighting the water. I know Steve is getting frustrated with me, as am I with myself. Back at the boathouse, I change my pitch back to the original numbers. At the dock before practice I moved my footstretchers one inch to the stern, effectively increasing the catch angle and decreasing the finish angle. This increases what is known as the turning moment. I can't wait to get back on the water and fix all of this mess. What better way to appreciate the blissful rows than to have experienced and learned from the crappy ones? If life was perfect how would we know?

Row Diary 5/15/07:

Nature's a mother. We rowed into a headwind this morning. With our oars loaded as they are, this makes for grueling, back-breaking work. Eight minutes into the first 15-minute piece and my heart rate is in the low 150's where it should be, but our splits show we are not moving the boat well. This is a valuable piece of information. Should we race into a headwind, we would use clams on the oars. A clam is a C-shaped plastic insert that goes on the oar collar. This increases the inboard and decreases the outboard of the oar, changing the mechanical efficiency. Using the car-hill analogy, if you want to maintain the same speed but the hill is getting steeper, you need to downshift. After that first piece, we practice a few race starts, called 5 and 5's. The first five strokes would not be dissimilar to running through the gears in a drag race. When you try to overcome the mass of the vehicle you are trying to move, you need a small gear. As the momentum of the mass increases you go to a bigger gear; the faster you go, the bigger the gear. In rowing, the racing start deals with variable stroke lengths to mimic gear changes. We usually use a progression of ¾, ½, ¾, full, full. Those are the first five strokes. The fractions refer to the length of the stroke or, more specifically, the depth of the leg compression. The second five to ten strokes are full power at an extremely high rate, about 41 to 42 spm. This morning we pull a 1:26 on our racing start. This is good. The speed is there; we just need to work "with" the boat/water/ourselves, not "against" the boat/water/ourselves.

Row Diary 5/18/07:

And so it all just seems to come together. This morning's row is fantastic. The set is good, the release is clean, and the catches are rock solid. Carl Prufer, our film-maker/rower buddy/fellow employee at the gym, has joined Ashland Rowing Club coach Joe Lusa in the launch. His idea is to amass a body of film about our training, that he might make a documentary of the whole process. Along the way, he will post segments on YouTube under the title *An Unlikely Pair*. With a rope around his waist for balance, Carl stands at the bow of the coach's launch, video camera firmly pressed to his eye, and begins his documentation of our journey.

Carl is a qualified companion in this adventure. He and Olympian Alfred Czerner won a Masters National Championship in the H category (70-74 years old) double sculls in 2006. I don't know if anyone else showed up that day, but I've got a really cool photo on my gym wall that proves that *they* did. But that is not what qualifies him. Carl has passion for many things; soccer, film, rowing, beautiful blondes and impossibly small English roadsters, to name a few. Admirable passions all, but that is not what qualifies him. At 70 chronological years old, Carl has an ageless sparkle in his eye and a genuine sense of wonder. When he is fired up about something, anything, it consumes him. He flashes a smile that transports me; suddenly we are both 12 and have discovered firecrackers for the first time. That is what qualifies him.

Today our steady-state work is in the 26 to 28 strokes per minute range. Amidst the scullers we pull away. We are moving the boat well. After the first piece, we practice race starts, which are a bit ragged at 41 spm. We take one last 5 and 5 to clean things up a bit.

A "power ten," "twenty," or any other number is a cue to bring focus to your power for that given number of strokes. It can also be used to focus on even a single element of the stroke, a "concentration ten" or a "ten for length," "ten for breathing," etc. On our last 20-minute piece we take power tens every 40 strokes.

In the final stretch we opt for a series of power twenties and really lay into it. In that moment in space and time we are utterly locked in and connected- to the boat, to the water, to each other. Controlled, efficient, relaxed and powerful, in that moment we fly. The universe shrinks and my consciousness expands and everything slows down and becomes quiet. This is my Zone. This is my God. Maybe this is my God Zone. I know forever that this is why rowing is my religion, offering me a glimpse of something, within and without myself, far beyond the ordinary. Steve extends his hand backwards and we shake. The violent ballet has begun.

4. THE PREP

5/20/07: First steady-state piece at 28 spm this morning. An Ashland Rowing Club men's quad is out with us this morning, made up of former National team and Masters National Championship guys. They give us a head start, maybe too much. We move through the body of Emigrant Lake. I begin to ease off as Steve makes the broad starboard turn into the arm and the dreaded headwind. Up to that point we have an excellent view of the quad as they gradually shorten the distance between us. Now at 28 spm, we are not letting off. Long and strong. Long and strong. The quad will not catch us today.

So now we set up to do our first interval training of the season. 30 strokes, roughly 250 meters. Rest and repeat 5 times. Our first piece is a mess. A fast mess, but a mess just the same. The rate seems absurdly high and I am getting pulled around. A well-rowed pair is a symbiosis of power between two people. Once that balance of power is upset, it becomes a tug of war and no one wins (although I make a mental note never to get in a tug of war with Steve). The next piece is pretty much the same; fast but terribly inefficient, painful, and out of control. By the third piece I feel as if I am just hanging on, desperate and overwhelmed. It is too early in the year to be effective at 37 spm and higher. Also, we are using race starts for these pieces. Also, I'm sitting behind a complete maniac. In a sprint scenario with a race start, it is easy to go out at a high rate and just stay up there. What we need to do is change our reality, both physically and mentally. Steve suggests we take the next piece "off the paddle". This means that instead of a high-intensity race start we take 5 strokes at a normal pressure and rate. Instead of a fast and furious environment with speed for speed's sake, in which we have to "settle" down to an optimal rate, we will take "5 to build" up to race pace with power for speed's sake, creating a much more controlled environment. And just like that, the fourth and fifth pieces are what the first three should have been. 35 strokes per minute, 1:36 split average. Strong and confident, symbiosis of power restored, wonder twin powers reactivated.

I met my wife at a Super Bowl party in San Francisco. She was intelligent, confident, artistic, expressive, and beautiful. An MBA working for a fortune 500 company, I was duly impressed. After the game, which the 'Niners won, of which we never saw even a single play, I walked her to her car. She said, "It was a pleasure meeting you." I wanted to say, "No the pleasure was all mine. Possibly you might join me for lunch tomorrow. We can continue our discussions on art and music and you can tell me your dreams and I will tell you mine and we will fall madly in love and isn't this fish excellent?" What I said was, "Yes it was." Yes it was? I turned and ran, hoping to be T-boned by a bus before reaching the nearest bridge to jump off. I had a few in the vicinity to choose from.

While we were still dating, I would awaken at 4:00 a.m. to leave Denise's San Francisco apartment, cross the Bay Bridge, and make practice in Oakland by 5:00 a.m. Denise would later tell me that she thought rowing was just a phase for me. She thought I would get it out of my system and move on. Of course that didn't happen. I hope it never does. I don't ever want to get rowing out of my system, and my mental image of "moving on" involves a pasture and a setting sun, or worse. Over the last 12 or so years I can say, with absolute confidence, that of our ten to fifteen most popular marital argument topics, Crew is in the top 5. Denise was not about to join the crew widowhood. That being said, we manage to strike a balance between crew, family, career and the entire minutia that come with those facets of life. Not that it has always been smooth, but it has never been dull and the fun quotient has always been extremely high.

Steve and I are no strangers to training for long periods of time toward a specific event. We have trained for master's national championships, world games, even the FISA master's world championships. We have raced successfully in and out of our age category. What makes this train ride different is that master's racing is 1000 meters. Olympic racing is 2000 meters. That's twice as long for all of you athletes. The physiological demands are dramatically different. With the exception of the San Diego Crew Classic, I haven't rowed a 2K since college.

5/21/07: Scary. Today I row a thirty-minute cat 6 slog today with Steve. Funny thing happened on the way to monotony.

Steve says, "So, we're sloggin' today?"

I say, "Yep."

He says, "What are we gonna do this at?"

I say, "1:58 to 1:59, something like that."

Consider this: the difference in split of 1/10 of a second would mean ½ meter per 2 minutes. So after 30 minutes, that 1/10 of a second discrepancy would amount to about 7 meters. A one second difference in split would amount to about 65 meters after 30 minutes. After our individual clocks had wound down to zero, we checked our monitors. Both were identical – 24 spm, 1:57.9, 7634 meters. Identical. Scary.

5/22/07: Water work was just kind of blah this morning, not much to write home about other than the water was stunning. Tuesdays are not regular turnout days, so the lake is silent; no launches, no coaches yelling, no coxswains barking commands from neighboring boats. We row right through the middle of the food chain — osprey above, trout below, shifting stroke rates from 24 to 26 to 28 every 3, 2, and 1 minutes. On the way back we shift every minute. Then it is off to the weight room for squats, seated rows, military presses, and abs. Tomorrow we will take a day off in preparation for a 2000-meter erg test.

Given the global population, the 2000 meter erg test is a concentrated piece of hell known by precious few – mostly junior and collegiate rowers. Carrie Graves, 1984 Olympic gold medalist and Texas Longhorn crew coach, refers to rowing in its most basic element as "pain management." I refer to the erg as a harbinger of pain, repetition and a profound longing to be anywhere else; the athletic equivalent of working at McDonalds. An ergometer is, by definition, a device to measure muscle power output. In 1980, Concept 2's Dreissigacker brothers put out the first rowing specific ergometer, now known simply as the erg.[2]

[2] To add insult to injury, a bunch of guys (and girls), calling themselves the CRASH-B's (Charles River Association of Sculling Has-Beens) decided to use the erg as a vehicle for racing. To break up the monotony of winter training in Boston and, coincidentally, the year of the Olympic boycott, Tiff Wood, Dick Cashin, Jake Everett and Holly Hatton held the first "indoor regatta." What started with twenty people now draws thousands from around the world every February.

This is my synopsis of a 2k erg test. You invite the grim reaper into your home for whiskey and cards. You drink too much and become belligerent, saying atrocious things about Mr. Reaper's dear mother. You then spout off about how you are the greatest and mightiest swinger of sickles ever, and that all others are weak and cowardly by comparison. At about this time Grim notices the extra card up your sleeve.

You have insulted Death, challenged Death and tried unsuccessfully to cheat Death. You are now feeling a bit nauseous and faint, due in part to the whiskey and in no small part to the fact that you are staring at an ass kicking of biblical proportions that you invited over in the first place. The ensuing retribution is a 2k erg test.

5/24/07: Wow. All of that stuff I said about the erg and the Grim Reaper while trying to be witty and clever for you dear readers? *It's all true.* Don't do it. Turn and flee while you have the chance. The Dreissigacker brothers are not your friends. They are selling Evil in a box, shipped direct, UPS, from Morrisville, Vermont. Man, what a train wreck. Went out too hard in the first 500 meters of our 2k test, landed in the pain tank by 750, started to get that sense of panic and losing control as my split began to slip, and then I did the very worst thing imaginable. I did the thing that your brain, heart, lungs, muscles and evolutionary hard wiring are demanding that you do, but that you are not supposed to do. I stopped.

Even though the ergometers are not physically connected, there is a connection between Steve and me. Much the same as fish within a school respond to the fish on either side of them, my stopping has an impact on Steve. Within another 250 meters he stops. This is not good. This is an utter failure. Now we are going to have to do this damn thing again and it's my fault. We take a 5-minute rest, and Steve puts duct tape over my monitor so that only the meters and the stroke rate show. "We're going to do this one at a time" he says. "I'll coach you and you coach me." Oh, well that's just … swell. Expending as much energy as we did on that first failed attempt did not help matters, but Steve's idea is that you just have to get through it, actually complete the distance, and not worry about the numbers. After all, neither of us has done many 2k erg tests in the last, oh, 15 years. Kill one demon at a time. He is right. Right still hurts.

I call Fritz to report on the general suckiness of my piece. We have been training predominantly low-intensity aerobic systems up to this point, so this first 2k should just be a benchmark, nothing more, he assures me. We will begin to add in more interval work, then retest in three weeks.

And just like that, Fritz has saved me, wiped away my sins; granted me a temporary reprieve. Live to fight, to perpetuate the lie, to chase Olympic coat tails another day.

5/25/07: It is nice to be back on the water, still licking my wounds from yesterdays sound thrashing. Again we are moving the boat well. 4 minute on, 6 minute off pieces and we are cruising in the mid 1:50's. Today there are five singles and a men's 4+ on the water. Today all are behind us but Scott in the single. Today we catch Scott. Nothing magical about it, just putting the blade in the water and applying pressure, consistently. Steve will go down to Santa Cruz to see his brothers and his Dad this weekend. We could use a little break, as we are both feeling a bit beat up and run down. I've got an old Ford tractor that I'm restoring, so I look forward to tinkering.

I am floating through life. I don't mean that in some lofty, metaphorical sense. As I am standing in the middle of the Ashland Food Co-op trying to decide between coffee, cottage cheese, salad, or a muffin (I compromise and get all of them), I feel like I am back in college. I have just come from practice, my hands are numb and swollen, my legs are tingling and there is a slight buzzing in my ears. I am just standing there, disconnected, floating in a separate space. Today I am acutely aware of my separate reality, so I stop to take a look around. I am not hurting anyone, at least not yet. In fact I feel quite invisible. I hold my face in my hands and rub vigorously.

I put my hands on my head and take a deep breath, just as my coach made me do while running stadiums at Humboldt State. I just don't remember recently feeling that disconnected from my physical surroundings, like a dream state, and I want to appreciate that singular, insulated, selfish, exhausted place for a moment. I feel like I could take a savage beating and not lift a hand to defend myself, but if I were dropped into a boat I would pull until I was told to stop or died. "Anyone with unlimited strength and courage can do it."

Whenever I felt that I had accomplished something worthy of his praise and brought it to his attention, one of my Dad's stock responses was, "Of course. Anyone with unlimited strength and courage can do it." This was the super hero way. While he never punished failure, he expected no less than full measure.

My best 2,000-meter erg score at Humboldt was 6:18. Most of the national team guys at the time were pulling between 6:00 and 6:10. Todd Stone and I had lofty plans of moving to Boston, working for Gentle Giant and training for the national team. The Gentle Giant Moving Company hires rowers for their strength and, in return, allows flexible schedules so they can train. This would be a foolproof plan. Todd and I, individually, were confident able-bodied happy-go-lucky collegiate rowers. Todd and I together were positively, notoriously foolish. This was a plan for us. Life had another plan for me. My dad had barely survived the Oakland firestorm of October 1991. My mom had not. After a year in both the Alta Bates burn unit and Golden State Rehabilitation Center, with no home or wife of forty years to come home to, he was going to need some help. Fingers and toes were missing. Expressive, dancing eyes and strength of character remained stalwartly intact. The road ahead would require unlimited strength and courage. There would be pain and suffering and grieving and tears. He never complained - not once.

5/29/07:   Dear Diary, I hope Timmy asks me to the homecoming dance … Actually I just have this journal documenting our training. Denise begs me to change Timmy to Sally. I argue that it would not be stereotypically correct, that in my Rockwellian allusion men do not keep diaries. But, as I tell my son, if you have to explain the joke it probably isn't that funny to begin with.

We row a straight four this morning with Don Daman and Scott Knox. A straight four has no coxswain and is written as "4-". A four with coxswain is written as "4+", and so on. We row a beat-up old Filippi knock off called "Lisa Ann." Our club picked it up from Sacramento State University what seems like too long ago for it to be any good — should probably take it out to the middle of the lake and shoot it. But we could not bribe a coxswain to show up at 5:30 a.m. so here we are.

As we carry oars to the dock, Don remarks, "It looks like a mirror out there". 5:30's mirror can be 6:00's maelstrom. And so it is this fine morning. Rounding the corner to the arm, we are greeted with wind, waves and whitecaps. This is going to be ugly.

At 26 spm, things get heavy fast. If we stop, we might swamp. If we try a broad port turn, we would probably get broadsided and roll. Even in May, this is still snowmelt. Over the howl and the spray Steve yells, "Keep going!" We whoop and holler and dig in for an epic battle of man against nature. Actually, it is just four guys rowing a boat on a lake into a headwind but, man alive, is it fun! After making it up the arm of the lake we rest and laugh at our triumph. Then, with a massive tailwind, we practically surf home.

The real beauty in this event is how it came together, *because we showed up*. Because the Lisa Ann is a battle-worn barge, because we have no coxswain to lose their nerve and weigh us down, because we have the four most experienced sweep rowers together, because rowing the pair this morning would have been stupid if not tragic, because we embrace the changes in our reality rather than fighting them, we get the religion and the philosophy. We get the row-life parallel. We get the violent ballet!

5/31/07: Andy's maximum power output 841 watts.

Steve's maximum power output 926 watts.

Maximum power on the ergometer is measured in watts relative to bodyweight in kilograms. The National Team standard for power output is a factor of 9. Currently at 92 kilos, my standard is 828 watts. At 100 kilos, Steve would need to pull 900 watts. The Olympic standard is 10 and higher. Eleven months to go.

6/1/07: Rowed a series of 4-minute pieces, followed by a 1,000-meter piece, in the pair against Scott and Eric in the double. They are also in their late forties and man, are they fast. Twice as many oars on the water, faster boat. Eric is a former national team rower and Scott has at least a half dozen master's regional and national championships under his belt, so it will be exciting to see those guys race in Canada this year.

6/3/07: We met at the boathouse at 5:30 a.m. to review film from Friday's workout. Scott points out that I am still dropping my outside elbow at the finish. Today we row our Ashland Rowing Club Men's Masters 8+. We will race this boat at the USRowing Northwestern Regional Championships next month.

One of the great things about rowing is the people who make up the sport. Rowing becomes the common thread that connects what might otherwise be eight unassociated individuals. In this boat we have two lawyers, two engineers, a writer, a trainer, a vet and a biologist.

It is painfully obvious that there is a joke in there somewhere. Feel free to write your own and send it to me.

6/4/07: Steve and I looked at film today. It appears that Steve's footstretchers, the boards that his feet are attached to, are set too high relative to his seat height. This would prevent him from getting enough forward body angle to achieve sufficient "reach" without compromising his low back, yet another variable to tweak and fine tune.

Today we do a modified 30-minute, category 6 slog on the ergs at the Medford gym, rowing by feel rather than heart rate. At 23 - 24 strokes per minute, Steve averages 1:55, I average 1:56.5. Next to us on another erg sits Marilyn. Marilyn is a member of our gym, not a rower, probably about 5'4" and in her mid-60s. She is already rowing when we sit down to begin, and has established her rhythm free of ego or expectation. She continues this rhythm without influence from the two meatheads next to her. Marilyn is consistent. Marilyn knocks out a 30-minute piece like a metronome. Marilyn has lost seventy pounds, and Marilyn is my hero.

6/5/07: This is a light weights week so we add a power workout on the ergs this morning. In a power workout the damper is set on #10, the work period is ten seconds and the rest period is 60 seconds. Power is measured in watts. The damper on a rowing ergometer changes the load dynamic. It doesn't actually change the resistance, but how you apply your power. The damper settings range from #1 to #10. #1 is like rowing a sleek racing shell, skimming across the water in halcyon tranquility as a Schumann concerto rises and falls through the mist, rising, and the leaves, falling, around you. #10 is like rowing a dump truck while mobsters with thick Jersey accents beat on you with pipes because you are trying to row off in one of their dump trucks. The goal is to pull at least 90% of peak power during the ten-second work period. This is repeated twenty times. As we are both able to pull greater than 90% peak power for all twenty pieces, this indicates that we need to retest our peak power. Oh joy.

For the afternoon workout I do some 500-meter intervals. Interval work is a great way to play in the pain tank, but jump out before it gets too ugly. The only rule is that the last interval must be as fast if not faster than the first interval. This teaches the psychological side of rowing, the pain management side. My workout consists of four times 500 meters with 3 minutes' rest in between. My fourth interval is 3/10 of a second faster than my first, so all is well. Or I'm just slacking in general, but the metaphysical implications of that statement make my brain hurt and my nose bleed, so I'm just gonna call it a day and be happy.

6/7/07: Bring on the demons. This morning's workout is a warm-up followed by two 1000-meter sprints with 5 minutes' rest. The real work comes in the afternoon. We set the ergs up in the parking lot at the Medford gym. Today's carnage is five times 500 meters with 3 minutes' rest. Again, the idea is to remain consistent from first piece to last. Without fail, this is how these things go — the first piece you get the kinks out, get your breathing settled, and get dialed in. The second and third pieces are usually your best efforts; you are warmed up, acclimated, and confident. You start the fourth piece with those same qualities. About 200 meters in, your reality begins to shift. You go to another, less hospitable place. It is a tide of pain. With every stroke, every ebb and flow, it washes over a little more of you. You cannot stop the tide as you sink in deeper and deeper. The walls close in. You fight for breath. There is ringing in your ears and the hint of nausea. As the hydrogen accumulates faster than your body can get rid of it, your muscles begin to lock up. Your stroke begins to shorten as your body collapses in on itself. You are submersed in the pain tank with 100 meters to go. What you do now defines you. Fight or flee. Today it is fight.

That fourth piece was everything that you had. You left it all right there in the parking lot. There is no fifth piece. How could there be? There is nothing left. This is the reality. How can you ask for something that doesn't exist?

I lied. I lied to you and I lied to myself. I had to. It was a coping mechanism. The truth is that it is the fifth piece that defines you. The reality is that there will be a fifth piece. How can that be if your reality says there is nothing left? These two realities can not coexist. Either you don't do the fifth piece or you find another gear. The fifth piece can't not exist. Therefore, you have to take control of your reality, which brings us right back to metaphysics. Damn, rowing is hard. My demon's done. Today I win.

No rowing this weekend. Denise and I took off to motorcycle through the Kalmiopsis wilderness to the Oregon coast. We had a wonderful trip on some potentially treacherous roads where Denise impressed me with her skills. She took her first ride more than a decade ago at the Lake Chabot parking lot in Oakland, California. Now she is beaming as she drags her footpeg for the first time in a steep corner 4000 feet above the Pacific Ocean. Motorcycling has many of the same elements as rowing; a marriage of speed and skill and wonderful external stimuli to let you know where you are in space and time.

6/12/07: We row a series of 3 minute on, 5 minute off intervals in the pair this morning. As of this date 34 to 35 strokes per minute seems to be optimal for us. We will build up to 37 spm in due time.

6/13/07: I meet Tammy Achurra at the boathouse this evening for some interval work. She is racing at the Northwest Regional's and has not yet submitted a 1000-meter erg score. The club standard for the women's racing team over 50 years of age is 4:30 or less. Without the age handicap it is 4:20. In 2005 she pulled 4:14.1. Last year at this time she pulled 4:09.7.

Today Tammy does three intervals of 1 minute 24 seconds on and 3 minutes off. Each interval represents one-third of a 1000-meter piece assuming a time of 4:12. This is a good way for her to reacclimatize herself to the pain, speed and mechanics of erg testing. Tammy had taken some unexpected time off and needs confirmation that she can still do this at the level she expects of herself. Based on her splits, this should serve as a valid confidence builder. I anticipate that her test would land her in the same range as last year, and even if she fell off the pace a bit, she would still be well below 4:20.

6/14/07: This morning for no particularly good reason I decide to do 300 meter sprints with 200 meters on the paddle (erg workout). "On the paddle" means rowing with little or no pressure. Five of these net me 2500 meters. My daughter woke up at 1:00 a.m. to cry about wanting to cuddle with mommy. When my 4:30 a.m. alarm goes off, I am feeling tired and beat up as I check to see that spine and ribs are in working order. I am restless as I head to the gym 15 minutes early.

The 7/12 pair workout was hard, maybe harder than I had realized. This morning we talk about cutting back on the training volume a bit. This is probably smart. This afternoon I will do a light piece. Tomorrow's water workout should be vicious in its intensity. Three times 500 meters — all out. This will definitely be one of those "go big or go home" workouts, low volume high intensity.

I do a light 4000 meters on the erg, heart rate below 135 bpm. Sleep cannot come too soon and, of course, it doesn't.

The adage, "love what you do and you will never work a day in your life" has not been lost on me. Before I learned to trust and empower my employees I worked as many as sixteen hours a day. Now with two facilities in Oregon and a second company licensing our medically based exercise system internationally, my short day is nine hours and my longest, Tuesday, is thirteen. Rowing is really just an extension of what I do for a living. Work, play, and religion are one and the same.

6/15/07: Everyone seems pretty amped this morning. Small boats - pairs, singles, doubles, will row three times 500 meters. A barnburner of a workout and we tear it up. Our numbers are excellent; we are relaxed and powerful. Most importantly at this point in time, it feels very controlled. With the August goal to be sub 3:30 (1:45 splits) in the 1000 meters in Canada, today's 500's are very encouraging – 1:41 to 1:44 without headwind, 1:46 to 1:47 with headwind, and 1:39 to 1:41 with a slight tailwind. We also row effectively at 36 strokes per minute, which is a pleasant surprise.

This afternoon Tammy will come in to do her 1000-meter erg test. We were talking about the psychological elements of racing. There are so many mind games that come in to play before a race or a test piece. What Tammy pointed out so affably was that if you spend all of your time worrying about and fearing the "what if" and the "this is going to hurt" then, before you know it, the race is almost over *and you weren't even really present to experience it!* Based on that row-life parallel epiphany, Tammy says, "Damn it, with all that I have invested in this sport, I want to be there for every stroke." Hmm, let's just let that sit for a moment.

One year ago this week at the Northwest Regional Championships, Tammy noticed a lump in her throat. Fellow club member Dr. Deborah Gordon convinced her to get it checked. It was cancer. Demons come in different shapes and sizes. One year, two surgeries, chemo, and a big fat life-altering curve ball later, here she sits at the erg, ready for battle. This 1000-meter erg piece will send a message, a butterfly effect that I hope to make bigger by repeating it. I give the commands, "Eyes closed ... deep breaths ... sit ready ... attention ... *row.*" With all that you have invested in this sport, you want to be there for every stroke. Tammy rows a 4:12.2. I tear up with pride. Tammy is my hero.

"There are those who live for the moment. There are those who live in the moment. Both may love to win. Both may race as hard as they are able on race day. Sometimes those who live for the moment win, but more often those who live in the moment win. Living in the moment means every day counts like race day, each piece on the water has meaning. Every person on the team adds to the forward momentum we are creating as we go. The momentum of this forward motion I call "success." In my experience in rowing, what I care to remember is the quality of the shared experience, in the quality of the moments, experienced in the moment.

You've heard the expression: "rising to the occasion." But, I ask: to what occasion should we "rise"? Isn't the entire process the occasion? Isn't it in the doing of it, in all the preparatory and participatory particulars, the occasion of the quality to which we aspire? When asked "why crew," I think that the answer lies in the quality of the time we create practicing and racing as one continuously evolving moment, awake, aware, and alive – in the moment. It's a place we regularly go to make something as it should be. And when medals follow it is all the sweeter."   – Jim Sims

5. BENCHMARK #1 – NW CHAMPIONSHIPS

6/17/07: Back in the four this morning. What a blast. Steve and I have been rowing with Scott and Don for a number of years now. We pride ourselves in not taking it too seriously. The fact that we got in the boat together twice before a regional championship is testament to that. Last year at the same event, we won our heat quite easily. I think that Pocock Rowing also won their heat. I do remember thinking, as we were setting our shell in the water for the final, that the Pocock guys looked *much* bigger and *much* younger than us. That six-lane final for the regional championship was a two-boat race between our Ashland Rowing Club 4+ and the Pocock 4+. We won by .89 second. The rest of the field was between 12 and 28 seconds back. I suspect that those fine gentlemen from Seattle will be looking for us this weekend to avenge that loss. I rather suspect that they thought they were going to win it. After all, who and where the hell is Ashland Rowing Club?

Anyway, this morning was big fun. We got up to 44 strokes per minute, which then made 39 spm bearable and 35 spm a stroll.

6/19/07: Our last day in the pair before Northwest Regionals. Today is race rehearsal, two 500-meter pieces with 5 minutes' rest in between. Hit it hard, be satisfied with the result, and leave it alone. Our first 500 has a race start; average split is

1:44.6 at 35 spm. Our second 500 is off the paddle; average split is 1:40.6 at 36 ½ spm. Anything under 1:45 is fine so all is well. We are where we are supposed to be. There is great peace and strength in feeling that you belong exactly where you are, right now.

6/22/07: Drove up to Vancouver, Washington for Northwest Regionals. Our first race was the B Pair (2-) at 6:21 p.m. Originally there were to be heats for this event, with the top three to qualify for the final. This is a good thing, as it gives you a chance to get your race jitters out, practice race strategy, check out your competition, etc. This year, however, USRowing recorded a new benchmark in race entries: more than 950. As a result, all small boat events would go to a timed heat/final scenario. In this case, the heat becomes its own final.

We figured that the pair from Pocock Racing would be our biggest threat. They were in lane 4 and we were in lane 5. We didn't know much about the other boats in our race, except that they all looked like they would get carded if they tried to buy beer after the regatta. I don't get carded much these days. This race would turn out to be a carbon copy of our pair final at the U.S. Masters Nationals in Seattle. Nervous, queasy, unable to focus, I am not mentally dialed in, not confident. At the start the water is choppy. We opt to go off clean instead of our usual 110% power start. This was mistake #1. Twenty strokes in and we still haven't settled, but we are pulling away from Pocock. As the field drops back, one other boat stays with us, way over in lane 1 or 2, I can't tell. At the 500-meter mark, where we would normally take a power 20, we are precariously close to the port buoy line. I back off a little, trying to get us back in the lane; mistake #2. The ghost ship across the field takes a seat on us. Damn it. We had talked about doing a 30-stroke "windup", increasing the rate every ten strokes, for our sprint. Down by a half of a deck length with 250 meters to go, we tried it. And that was mistake #3. That tactic assumes that we are rowing long with power and ratio. We are not. We are tight and jacked up. Rate increases need to come as a result of increased power output, not in spite of it. Now we lose ratio and length and probably go slower. The ghost ship takes their sprint with power, increasing length and ratio. Just like Nationals in Seattle, this turned out to be a two-boat race. And just like Nationals in Seattle, we settle for the silver medal. The ghost ship, from Sammamish Rowing, wins gold.

6/23/07: The 4+ Oarsman of the Apocalypse. Saturday morning we are at the racecourse at 6:00 a.m. for our heat in the men's C 4+. There are three heats, with the top two finishers from each going to the final. Kent Mitchell once wrote that the C 4+ is arguably the most competitive race in Masters rowing. Having won this event last year, as well as having had the privilege of winning a world championship in this class, I agree. Looking at our heat, and admittedly a numbers geek, I surmise that this is going to be a two-boat race between Lake Union and us.

We get hands on at 6:30, and conditions simply could not be any better; absolutely still and quiet. At water's edge, race officials check the boat and the coxswain's identification bracelet. Once past that inspection we are allowed on the water. This is our race. Our warm-up is as stable as a granite slab. All power is going straight to the water. Jitters give way to excitement. This is going to be a crush fest. We enter our lane and back it down to the stake boat, where one of the many volunteers takes hold of our stern. The nearest referee launch asks our coxswain, Beth Hoffman, to raise her hand. She does so. The ref radios the race tower. The race tower radios someone else. There is a pause. The omnipotent tower speaks, "Coxswain, you are wearing the wrong color bracelet. You did not weigh in this morning.

Ashland Rowing Club, you are disqualified and must leave the race course immediately." Hmm. How does this fit into the row-life parallel?

At this point I could tell you, in great detail, the distance and resonance with which swear words can travel over glasslike water. I could tell you of the conspiracy theories held that USRowing officials actually believe and continue to perpetuate the belief that Ashland Rowing Club coaches instruct their crews to ram other boats, and that this is one of the ways they keep us down. I will say this: the officials would not allow us to race and have the cox weigh in after the fact. They would not allow us to race as an exhibition. We even offered to give everyone else a 100-meter head start. That didn't go over too well. Once outside the course, we were not allowed to row at full pressure. We watched, powerless and motionless, as our race passed by within oars' reach.

Lake Union won the heat by 16.3 seconds over the rest of the field. After the boats had passed, we began to row. We were ordered to stop. When the official deemed it appropriate, we were allowed to paddle back. I felt like Buck in the *Call of the Wild*. My pride hurt. I was enraged to the point of tears and there was nothing I could do about it. We started to get quiet. We started to smolder.

The men's D 8+ heat was next. The rest of our boat could feel our intensity. They were feeding on it. This was a deep field. From California, there was Los Gatos and two Marin 8+'s. From Oregon, there was Tiff Wood's Willamette crew, Corvallis and Ashland. From Washington there was Vashon and Pocock. Finally, from Canada there was Drew Harrison's Victoria City crew. In the world of Masters rowing, this was heady stuff. On any other day this might be intimidating. On this day we were to be their apocalypse;

their grim reaper; their erg piece gone terribly wrong.

Our 3 man, Jay Schindler, put it best when he said, "That was a tie boat race ... for about five strokes." We were supposed to take a power 20 at the 500-meter mark. Beth abandoned that notion based on the space we had already put between the pack and ourselves. 525 meters. After all, it was top three to the final, right? 550 meters. *No, no, no, NO!* I was not done yet. 570 meters. I, no, we had something to say. We tried saying it before and it fell on deaf ears. 585 meters. I'm just getting started. 600 meters. *"Take the twenty,"* I scream. Beth responds, "OK, you want the twenty, we take the twenty in two, in one, *on this one.* We are frenzied. We drive that 20 so hard that there is no race course left for a sprint. We post the fastest time of both heats. Bowman Ron Iverson yells "Let this be a lesson to you. Don't piss off the stern four." Willamette and both Marin boats do not make the final.

We raced the final the same way we raced the heat, only 7 seconds faster, winning the Northwest Regional Championship with a time of 3:09.42 and upsetting the heavily favored Victoria City boat from Canada by 4.19 seconds. Our guys were so dialed in, so utterly focused to the task at hand, that any other outcome was simply not a part of our reality. Later that evening, Steve and I won the men's C 2-. That was nice, too.

So how does this fit into the row-life parallel? Profoundly, beautifully, perfectly really. When I rowed in college, Coach Jeff would ask us to "find the love" in what we did. Why else would we endure the hours of torture, day in and day out, morning and night, if we didn't love what we did? There is certainly no monetary benefit, no fame and adulation, so the reward must be intrinsic. In the competitive realm of collegiate athletics, we took that to the next level.

With a sharpie I penned a T-shirt that said "Find the Love ... and use that love to Crush Everything in your Path."

I didn't drive 300 miles to argue with referees, I came to row. Filing a protest after the fact won't give me my race back. Throwing a tantrum on the shore won't help either, and will make me look like an idiot to the impartial observer. I already do that enough on my own. But channeling that energy into some other more productive form of self expression, like the next race (which I do have some control over) seems to work quite nicely. Maybe if we had raced the C4+ heat and final we would have been too tired to row such an epic upset in the D8+ which, in the larger rowing communal sense, casts both a broader and more poignant shadow for the Ashland Rowing Club. So the row-life parallel is this — when life gives you lemons, crush them and smash them and rip them into little bits and then reshape them into a steak and a cold beer. Life is too short for lemonade. Yes, that quip reeks of macho hubris. Not to worry. It will pass.

Kathy Frederick founded Row for the Cure to benefit the Susan G. Komen Breast Cancer Foundation. As a sort of publicity stunt, she has rounded up a bunch of former National team and Olympic rowers for a 1,000-meter relay race in single sculls and Steve has been invited. The idea is that the first leg will sprint 250 meters. Then the middle leg will sprint 250 meters, make a 180 degree turn without flipping, then sprint back 250 meters. When that person crosses the line from where they started, the anchor leg will sprint the final 250 meters. Then all will cheer in the name of Row for the Cure and life will be good. I'm thinking a camera will be in order for such an occasion. The chance of Steve flipping a single at full pressure with a 180-degree turn is probably pretty high and that would definitely be a Kodak moment for the ages. Steve doesn't have quite the same vampire-to-sunlight response to sculling that I do, but he's not far behind.

As we walk along the shore passed the finish line tent and the staging area Steve seems calm, too calm. "So, are you ready for this thing?" He says, "Sure." Hmm. OK, I guess that just is what it is. I would have thought he would be more nervous or at least more excited than this. It's almost as if he knows something that I don't.

Steve says "How about you?" Uh oh.

"How about me what?" This could be bad.

"Are you ready?" What has he done?

"What have you done?" Steve's smile is starting to break through. He can't maintain the cool act any longer.

"I told them we would race the pair. You didn't think I was going to scull this thing, did you? I'm stupid, but I'm not that stupid!"

The odds of getting the leg with the 180-degree turn are exponentially proportionate to the odds of flipping at the 180-degree turn in a pair – not the weapon of choice for a single sculls race. Clearly this idea is too stupid to pass up, which is what makes Steve so wise. We get the turn, which is as it should be. We do not flip. We also get the reward of showing up, having a great time and getting a bitchin super nifty pink backpack for our efforts. I think my daughter will take ownership of that one.

At the line before the start, a National team sculler next to us asks if we are going to the trials. We say yes. She says, "Make sure you bow to Volp." She is referring to Bryan Volpenhein. I make a mental note of things to do when I go to the Olympic trials – don't forget my trou, bring Cytomax and sunscreen and an extra water bottle, stay off my feet, bow to Volp; got it.

6/26/07: There is no doubt we are feeling a bit beat up after this weekend. Go figure. This morning we go out for a low rate, full power, steady state, 19 spm, and everything is just wrong. The steering is wrong, the foot stretchers are wrong, I'm getting pulled around, Steve is frustrated, and a hard workout is getting harder by the minute.

Ah, perspective.

We resign ourselves to get rid of the rudder altogether and change the rig sternward. Back to the boathouse and off to weight room. Then back on the ergs for low rate power pieces in the afternoon, the third workout of the day. I doubt the national team guys are taking a break, so neither will we. I'm feeling better already.

Virgil Butler forgot to grow up. His wife Marian probably told him to numerous times. He may have even planned to get around to that at some point, but he kept getting distracted by all of the fun stuff to do in this life. Virgil is both funny and wise. In true Yogi Berra fashion, Virgil pointed out to me, "The fit people that you see exercising at the gym are the ones that need it the least," he feigns ignorance and, with a sly smile asks, "Why is that?"

In 1947 Virg pitched for Cal in the first collegiate World Series against Yale University. He struck out Yale's team captain, George "Poppy" Bush, to win the series. "The future president couldn't hit a curve ball," Virgil is fond of saying. In 1948 he signed a pro contract with the Oakland Oaks baseball team, "for just enough to pay my fraternity bill." Marian told him that, as long as he could win 20 games per season, he could play ball with his friends for a living. True to his word and his beautiful bride, he hung up his glove with a two-season record of 31-16 and moved on to other adventures. At 87 years young he still exercises 3 to 4 times per week, plus pool classes; still goes out to breakfast with the fellas on Wednesday mornings. When I opened my gym in Ashland he gave me a plaque that read, "There is no special age in life for launching a new dream. The perfect time to begin is always today." It is precisely that kind of attitude that keeps Virgil ageless. I am grateful to have him as a friend.

6/27/07: Oh …. my …. *gawd,* I feel like road kill. I am absolutely wiped. There is no specific pain, just numbness and bone deep fatigue. 2000 meters into a 4k erg piece and I just stop. Everything is seizing up. I am not functioning properly. I call Steve to whine about my sad condition. He is exhibiting identical symptoms.

Ed McNeely's voice echoes in my head. "It's not that you can't *do* the work that the young guys are doing, it's that you can't *recover* as fast as they do." Fritz said, similarly, if we were training with the national team, when they would be heading out at 5 p.m. for their third workout of the day, we would be better off skipping that session in favor of rest and recovery. So maybe some days, instead of three-a-days, we just do the morning water work, then the weight room work. This of course would be (I know you can see this one coming, I set it up so obviously. Here it comes, it's a slow ball) the *one a day plus iron.* Old guy humor. Quality over quantity; train smart.

6/29/07: Today we just may have found another gear. Foot stretchers moved, rudder removed, it feels like a different boat. We fly. Sunday we will attempt to capitalize on these adjustments with a series of timed pieces. The idea is to row a series of pieces all out, then make small changes to the rig and repeat the piece and continue to fine-tune until we have the optimum setup. If the boat slows down we reverse the changes. If it speeds up, we continue to tweak until it slows down.

7/1/07: Major breakthrough today. We continue to adjust our foot stretchers to the stern. It is not enough to pull hard. When you are generating peak power it has to reach the water effectively. Without effective application, power is useless. So the key is to align yourself, when mechanically in the most powerful position, with the oar, when it is mechanically in the most powerful position, relative to the water. What we found out was that our power was coming on late in the stroke. We had already adjusted once and were faster for it. We adjusted again. We were faster. We adjusted again. We were faster. Six weeks ago we were pulling 1:39 splits at 33 strokes per minute. Today we are pulling 1:34 to 1:35 splits. On the final piece we pull a 1:29 split at 35 spm. That is not slow.

7/6/07: The spinal tap workout. This morning we do a series of minute on/ minute off pieces. These are done in a series of pyramids, with the stroke rate going from 30, to 32, to 34, to 35. Two rounds net us eight pieces. The ninth and tenth pieces are done at 35-36 spm. After the ninth piece I am in a world of hurt. Number ten will be a character builder. I fear it only briefly, and then embrace its inevitability. That, in and of itself, is empowering. The sun is up now. It is hot at 6:30 a.m. We are drenched, doubled over in the boat and heaving. I get the handshake. The tenth piece is done. This was a good workout.

Paddling back to the dock it is quiet; too quiet. Steve says, entirely too casually, "How ya feeling?" I say, "Fine" but I already know what is coming next. Like an old married couple, I beat him to it and ask, "We're going to do an eleventh piece, aren't we?" I already know the answer. Maintaining his casual act, Steve says, "You've seen the movie Spinal Tap, haven't you?" Just as there was a Volume 11 in Spinal Tap, there is a Piece 11 this morning. It is the eleventh piece that defines us…bring it.

"Rowing is a sport for dreamers. As long as you put in the work, you can own the dream. When the work stops, the dream disappears." – Jim Dietz

7/10/07: Today we had a training session with USRowing hall of fame Olympian and Coach Jim Dietz. What a breath of fresh air that was. After four years in the pair with no concentrated coaching, we have insulated ourselves through compensatory, "defensive" rowing. As Jim picks us apart, deconstructing and rebuilding, I realize that most of what he tells us is the same stuff that I tell my crews as a coach. How, then, could I possibly be guilty of the same things? One reason is that my kinesthetic awareness of what I am doing is compromised by sheer repetition without an objective eye to keep me in check. But if we represent the upper echelon of the food chain within our club, who is there to watch us? We are relatively big fish in an extremely small pond. In order to grow, we need to be picking fights with Great White Sharks off the coast of South Africa. Our younger counterparts on the U.S. National Team are getting this kind of input daily.

7/13/07: We have been thrashing ourselves on the ergs since our session with Jim Dietz, rowing 19 strokes per minute at full power. The low rating allows us to tap in to the load and really get the sense of accelerating into the finish of the stroke. Good clean wholesome vicious brutal gut wrenching fun. Sore sore sore.

7/16/07: More of the same. My back is in knots as I adapt to my "new" style of rowing. The world cup times in Linz, Austria are frighteningly fast. Great Britain, dead last at the 1000-meter mark, sprints for the win in the last 500 meters.

7/23/07: Steve had been in Kauai for a week. He rowed a rusty, salt encrusted model B erg out of one of the local outrigger clubs. I continued with the back breaking low rate erg work. Yesterday we were back on the water rowing full power at 15 to 16 strokes per minute. Brutal. Just brutal. I haven't had much to write about as it has been the same day in and day out; low rate, heavy, hard work.

7/25/07: Yesterday I woke up at my standard 4:45 and could barely get out of bed. I made it from the bed to the couch and crashed. I woke up at 5:25. Five minutes to get to the lake. I am beat. Beat up, beat down, just plain beat. Back to that college mentality of being numb, constantly sore and tired, but never stopping, always moving forward - Spartan.

We finish our first piece to the end of the arm; 16 spm full power. I am dreading the return piece. The first one hurt and I am wiped out. As we sit there, breathing, pooling in our own sweat, after these many years it is still impossible not to be affected by the beauty of this spot. Emigrant lake sits 2200 feet above sea level, between the Cascade and Siskiyou mountain ranges. Canada geese, osprey, bald eagle and today coyote share the real estate. Just over Siskiyou pass, between Pilot Rock and Mt. Shasta lays the Oregon/California border.

We talk about fast hands away at the finish and staying relaxed into the catch. And then it happens. After two weeks of frustration and pain and neuromuscular re-patterning, it clicks. Big, stable, powerful strokes. Every stroke begs for one more just like it, and then it comes. And then the next, and the next. It's as if we rowed through some portal into a parallel universe, but without the bad Star Trek haircuts and itchy polyester uniforms. Could this be the best row I've ever had? Could these be the best strokes I have ever taken? This is crazy. I don't remember ever feeling *just* like this. There was the Head of the Charles when our four seemed to skim above the water, and the world championship four that felt like the power might break the boat in two all the way to the last stroke (note: those two boats, four years apart, were the same athletes; me, Steve, Dave Potter and Eric Stevens). But this is the pair! This is huge! The hand of god, my rowing god, not to be mistaken with your god, but maybe, has reached out and gently tapped me on the shoulder. I am scared to stop, as I may never feel this again. I am scared to continue, as I might screw it up.

Like most life altering religious experiences, it takes a while to fathom what has taken place. Now a day later, I know in my heart and head that those were some of the best strokes I had ever taken. Is that really such a big deal? At the end of the day, at the end of our days, isn't it just rowing a boat on a lake? It is just that. It is also everything else. It is so much more. It is the universe on the head of a pin. I can't wait for Friday.

"Nice? It's the only thing, said the Water Rat solemnly, as he leant forward for his stroke. Believe me, my young friend; there is nothing – absolutely nothing – half so much worth doing as simply messing about in boats. Simply messing... he went on dreamily: messing about...in...boats; messing..."

— Kenneth Grahame, *The Wind in the Willows*

.

6. BENCHMARK #2 – CANADA

David Starr Jordan was a climber. In 1881, the first president of Stanford University climbed Switzerland's Matterhorn. It is said that Stanford's motto, "Die Luft der Freiheit Weht" (the Winds of Freedom Blow), was first uttered by Jordan during that epic climb. His Swiss guide recounted the statement to fellow guides who passed it on to the townspeople who translated it to German. The Stanford Alpine Club, however, has a slightly different account:

It is on his first ascent of the Matterhorn, one raw spring day, that Dr. Jordan is said to have uttered those famous words that subsequently became the stirring motto of the University he headed: Die Luft der Friheit [sic] Weht (the winds of freedom blow). However what Dr. Jordan actually said is "The wind is too damn cold;" this was mistaken by his Swiss guide as "The winds of freedom blow." Thus has an error committed on the heights of the formidable Matterhorn become the stirring motto of one of the great American Universities.

– Stanford

There is merit to disclaimers of this account, but it is a great story…

68 years later in 1949, Al Baxter and his climbing partner Bud Gates were back in Switzerland. Al was doing his graduate work at the University of Zurich. He graduated Stanford with a degree in philosophy in 1947, the same year he suffered nineteen fractures in his legs and ankles from a leader fall on Yosemite's Cathedral Spire.

Dad had impossibly good luck considering the situations he often found himself in. While boarding in a room on the second floor, he reviewed his studies with his tuxedo laid out and a bottle of champagne cooling in a bucket. He had been invited to a party that night and, as his mother had told him and as he would later tell me, 'never go anywhere without a tuxedo and a bottle of champagne." There was no running water in individual rooms when you were a border. Downstairs the widow who owned the house was performing some magical ritual of dry cleaning when the gas stove ignited. Dad was facing the window when it imploded, sending glass into his shirt and forearms and skull, sucking the fire towards him as it chased oxygen toward the broken windows. The explosion was massive, the widow near death. Dad popped the bottle of champagne, doused it over a bath towel and wore it as a shield and breathing apparatus. He made his way downstairs, found the body of the widow and carried her to survival. He never talked about it. As my mom would later tell me, the widow would most certainly have died had he not saved her.

In Zermatt, Al entered a shoe shop for hobnails. In those days the cutting edge of mountaineering technology was to screw hobnails into the soles of your boots for traction. The shoemaker told him that there was an Italian climber who had come up with a prototype for a mountaineering boot sole that was quite promising. So over the

Theodul pass went our intrepid heroes to meet with the Italian climber Vitale Bramani. I have read published accounts of what transpired between those men that day in 1949. It has been written that Baxter and Gates "bought" 100 hundred pairs of the soles. The version I heard growing up was more of a barter than a buy. It seems that while Bramani had something that Dad and the Stanford Alpine Club wanted, they had an abundance of nylon rope, which Italian climbers wanted.

A few hundred feet of rope lighter, but one hundred pair of climbing soles heavier, Bud and Al left Milan and trekked back over the Theodul foot pass to Zermatt. There they sold most of the soles to the shoemaker and local climbing guides (saving some to bring back to the States). With their profits they bought bratwurst and kirshwasser and stuck around long enough to climb the Hornli, Italian and Zmutt ridges of the Matterhorn, the Northwest face of the Breithorn and two routes of the Weisshorn. They were joined by my brother's future godfather Ulf Ericson (who would die in the 9/11 world trade center attack), Fearless Freddy Hubbard, and Nick Clinch.

The Stanford Alpine Club motto was "no guts, no glory." True to President Jordan's geographic and linguistic mishap, a parallel scenario had taken place. It has been said that Al Baxter and Bud Gates gave back to Zermatt what Zermatt had given to Dr Jordan. In that parallel vein, a Swiss guide looked at Nick Clinch's SAC card and smiled. *No guts, No glory* had been translated into German; "ohne Darme, kein Ruhm." The literal translation: *No sausage casings, no victory.* Ah, the more things change …

And what of the Italian climber who bartered the soles? I like to think that he was as gutsy and determined as my dad. He had lost 6 friends in a climbing tragedy that he felt could have been avoided with proper footwear. This was the event that fueled the passion behind his invention. On July 31st, 1954 a team of Italian climbers became the first ever to conquer K2, the second highest mountain in the world. They wore Dolomite boots equipped with Vitale Bramani's soles. While Baxter and Gates "imported" them via backpack to the States in 1949, they wouldn't be officially licensed in North America until 1965. Those soles are now known the world over as *Vibram*. Super heroes speak all sorts of languages.

8/5/07: We rowed the C 4+ with Scott and Don. First time back in the boat since the non-race at NW regionals. To explain the experience of that 4+, I am going to have to draw upon all of my literary powers to create for you, the reader, a whole picture, a sensory experience, a palate of emotions from which to scoop up larger than life size portions. Ok, here we go – *Still pretty darn fast.* Yep, that ought to do it.

More rigging adjustments. I have been talking with Mark McAndrews at Concept 2 about catch angles. Now, I know that you would love to read about catch angles for chapter upon chapter, but I will not indulge you. The short version is this: Concept 2's Fat Smoothie oar will handle a greater catch angle than other oars, allowing the athlete to "catch" more water. The problem is that it also creates a greater load for the athlete; so gearing becomes an issue again (remember the car and the hill?). Presumably the stronger the athlete the greater the load he or she can handle, but for how long, at what stroke rate, over what distance?

8/7/07: We change the inboard measurement of the oar to 116 cm and the spread to 86.5 cm and do a three times 500-meter workout. Fast and painful, as it should be. But could we hold that for 2000 meters? No, no way. The wheels would fall right off. With Canadian Masters Nationals next week, could we sustain that load for 1000 meters? I think we will try to find out. If we could just make the boat go straight!

8/13/07: I had been feeling pretty beat up these last few weeks. Back pain, knee pain and a nagging collarbone injury had also reared its ugly head. So I was quite pleased when, after yesterday morning's row with the men's 8+, everything felt like it was in its proper place. Ahhh.

The lane draws for Canada are up online, which is always exciting. Should be fun. "Should be fun," as well as "oh joy," are pair-speak for "I am trying to suppress the urge to go vomit in the bushes." But all in all I'm feeling pretty happy with my place in the universe as I squat down to take a wire brush to my dirt bike's engine block on Sunday evening. What better time to feel and hear a "pop" in my left lower back. Far enough away from disks and multifidi, I am relieved to experience no radiating or referred pain. What I am experiencing as the evening wears on is acute, white-hot contact pain. Oh joy

8/14/07: 30 stroke pieces with racing starts this morning. We row between Scott and Toni in a double and Corinne and Cindy in a pair. The idea is to get a sense of whether we are going straight or not. It works: we are not.

More adjustments and more tweaking. This will be our last water session before Canada. My back seems to be holding up, but guarded. I see Dr. Patty Frires and she prescribes me celebrex, skelaxin and vicodin. Between that and the Cytosport products, I will be crossing the border with a small duffel bag filled with pills and Ziploc bags containing white powder. It is quite obvious what the inference would be should customs agents inspect the contents of my bag. Do I even need to say what I would be labeled as given the state of the world today? I've got enough pressure in my life without being called a pro cyclist.

8/15/07: 5,000 meters on the erg this morning and my back held up well. When we get to Canada on Friday we will go out and practice in the lanes. Having never raced without a rudder, and having never practiced in lanes, and Friday being the day before the race, this would be smart.

8/16/07: Two times 250 meters, 1:30 rest to see how my back is holding up. 1:28.8, 1:26.8; I guess that's OK considering. It is now 11:37 a.m. In 14 hours and 23 minutes I will get up from a restless sleep, pick up Tammy, then Steve, and head for the airport. The forecast calls for rain and temps in the 50's in Victoria. If that keeps the wind down then so much the better.

All of the time that it takes to do this stuff, this training, can be divided into two camps. The first camp would be the gym workouts, erg training and weight training. This camp makes a fairly small impact on the rest of my life because that is what I would be doing anyway. Other than occasionally rescheduling clients to make room for our training, it doesn't impact the lives of the people around me: my family, friends and employees. I should add that I have a really hard time taking myself seriously when I say "employees". They are just really cool people who I admire and respect and the least I can do is pay them something to keep them hanging around and making me look good.

The second camp would cover water time and racing. This camp requires an incredible amount of support, time, patience, and sacrifice from everyone around me. Work schedules shift, calls are made at the last minute, other commitments are broken, weekends are stolen from Denise and Garrett and Aubrey, and the village bends over backwards to support its two village idiots.

8/20/07: Five events, five gold medals. Here is a recap of the Canadian Masters Nationals. We arrived Friday, rigged the pair and went out for a row on Elk Lake in beautiful Victoria, British Columbia. This would be our only chance to practice in lanes. The dock master informs us that we are *not* allowed to enter the lanes. Oops. Plan B is to row alongside the course and use the outside lane marker as a gauge. This works well enough, and the boat feels good. Mostly it's helpful for calming pre-race jitters. That evening we are asleep by 8:30 p.m. Saturday's first race is the men's C4+. This is perfect, as it will be a great warm-up for the pair race. It is also our chance at redemption for not getting to race at the Northwest Regional Championships. Lake Union is here, and we owe them a good battle. I honestly don't remember who else is in that race, and it really doesn't matter. This is a two-boat race from start to finish. We win by 4 seconds.

The pair, of course, is The Race. In our event is Lake Washington, the 2006 US champions in the A Pair, the San Diego pair that beat us at that same regatta, the Sammamish "ghost ship" that beat us at Northwest Regionals, and others to make up a seven-lane final – 3 Cs and 4 As. Fast company. I remember the start being fast and powerful. We go out furiously. It works. Immediately we and the Lake Washington pair jump ahead. They have a boat length on us. At the 250 it is only a half of a boat length. Legs burn, ears ring, eyes blur. By the 500 we have a boat length on them at 36 strokes per minute. We are in first place by a boat length over Lake Washington and open water over the rest of the field. First place hurts. I catch a massive crab (my blade dives deep in the water and gets stuck) and we come to a dead stop. It is a minor miracle that we do not flip. Lake Washington does not miss a beat and the rest of the field is fast approaching.

We pick it back up just passed the 500-meter mark with Sammamish, the ghost ship, moving toward us at a considerable clip. However bad it may have hurt to be in first, it hurts pretty darn bad to row a race, come to a violent and unexpected stop, and then start a race again. I don't know how we did it, by what means — guts, fear, anger, shame, a combination — but we managed to build up enough boat speed to hold off the field. As clearly as I remember the first 500, the second 500 is a nightmarish blur of pain and desperation. What was a race for first is now a fight for survival. This is rowing at its most primal. We cross the line second over all, 6.65 seconds behind Lake Washington, 2.28 seconds ahead of Sammamish, winning gold in the C class by 18.54 seconds.

Hmm. I caught a crab. There is a metaphysical rub here. One could ask the question "*How* did I catch a crab? It could have been anything; turning my head to look across the field at Lake Washington, catching the bottom of my blade during the recovery so that I enter the water at an angle (I think this is what happened), Steve making an adjustment and my reacting or not reacting to it. Maybe it is all of the above at exactly the same time. This was not a pretty row. The second half had considerable chop, sideways rollers and a headwind off the starboard bow. So any number of mechanical elements could have contributed.

The metaphysical question lurks in darker, murkier waters; *why* did I catch a crab? Did I impel the crab because I was too deep in the pain tank to survive, the equivalent of stopping during a 2k erg piece? Was the crab manifested because I was on course to break through a whole new ceiling of unknown potential that I was instinctually afraid of? Is this what primal fear is? I believe I will have the rest of my life to explore these questions. I believe this is why we are on this journey, why I write these pages. Says Nietzsche, "When one rows it is not the rowing which moves the ship: rowing is only a magical ceremony by means of which one compels a demon to move the ship." When Steve is backed into a corner, when a seriously big race is on the line, he basically snaps. He goes somewhere else, finds another gear that he normally doesn't use. I call it the demon gear. It's the place where Olympians go. I don't know the genetic password to get me in to that clubhouse. What truly sucks about this gear is that it's next to impossible to train for it. Everything just goes out the window and I fight for my life. Steve explains it this way, "I'm fuckin' nuts and I'm really, really strong." True. Harsh, but true.

Sunday we won the men's D4+, most notably against Tiff Wood, Bill Byrd and crew from Willamette Rowing. We then won the men's D8+ and a stroke for stroke slug fest with Lake Union Crew in the mixed C8+. This is an awesome boat that is always a joy to be in. One of the greatest things about this boat is it puts our men's C4+ right smack in the middle of the boat. This is called the Engine Room and is particularly suited for meatheads and hammers. Small-boat racing does not allow room for either. Being back in the Engine Room is like being home. I don't have to think. I have one job and that is to apply power, lots of power. We have absolute confidence in our stroke, Diane Green. Like soldiers, we follow her into battle with complete commitment. And not unlike soldiers, metaphorically speaking, we will die for her in the pursuit of our goal.

The other cool thing is that we never practice. *Never.* The boat just works. It's like an old friend that you haven't seen for a while, but you pick up right where you left off. It's organic, it has a great sense of flow, and it makes me proud of my Ashland Rowing Club.

We talk to Tiff in the parking lot. Tiff Wood is known infamously as "The Hammer". He gained this moniker through his somewhat unorthodox and brutal rowing style at Harvard and three consecutive Olympic teams. Christopher "Tiff" Wood is also, as mentioned before, one of the founding fathers of the CRASH-B indoor rowing championships. He and Steve both felt the sting of the 1980 boycott, although I rather doubt that common bond is strong enough to compensate for the Harvard/Yale rivalry between them. He thought the trials were a great idea and seemed genuinely enthusiastic. He said that he had thought of going to the doubles trials with Bill Byrd "just to beat up on the young guys for the first 400 meters, and then fall apart."

8/31/07: Okay, where to begin, post-race depression and physical recovery, tracking the World Masters Championships, this morning's awesome row (the fine art of surrendering yourself) or pair partner investments? Let's start with the World Championships. Why are they important?

In a pre-Olympic year, the World Championships are an Olympic qualifying event. In the men's pair, a country has to finish in the top eleven to be eligible to compete in the Olympic games. Kyle Larson and Jason Read are the U.S. pair. After making it through the heats and "reps" ("repechage" is French for *second chance*), they finish fifth in the Semifinal. This puts them in the B Final, which means as long as they don't finish dead last USRowing will qualify. This keeps our dream of going to trials alive.

Let me just go on record saying that, of the twenty-four countries entered in the Pair, my pick is Australia first, New Zealand second, and France, Great Britain and South Africa slugging it out for third. Having followed elite rowing for some years, I am not displaying great intuitive genius, rather pointing out what seems to be logically obvious. I also don't think anyone can *touch* the Aussies. They are amazing.

I have been muddling my way through post race issues of physical recovery and emotionally feeling like a bit of a train wreck. My third and fourth ribs on the left side have a habit of popping out, which locks up my left shoulder, which makes my back work overtime, which usually results in injury, which invariably pisses off my pair partner, which makes for crappy rowing, which upsets the universe.

The emotional side of things goes like this:

Imagine a timeline in the form of railroad tracks. This stretch of railroad-track timeline is 18 weeks long. The end of the line, at 17 ½ weeks, is Canada. You have a train, your very own locomotive. It is big and sleek and shiny and old school and ultimately quite fast and impressive. You are the sole driver, and there are no passengers. You could argue that your pair partner is on board with you but, for the sake of this metaphor, let him get his own choochoo. Your locomotive has one speed and that is full speed. But locomotives, because of their massive size, take time to get up to full speed. This particular locomotive takes 17 ½ weeks to get up to full speed. You stomp on the Go pedal with all your might and the locomotive lets out a sigh and inches forward, creaking and straining and steaming under its own mass. On your railroad timeline inches are minutes, meters are hours, a quarter-mile is a day, and a mile is a week. So you inch along and the creaking and straining and steaming eases and feet per second become miles per hour. 2, 3, 4, 5 miles per hour. 10, 15, 20 miles per hour. The clanking and bouncing and rattling are more pronounced from 25 to 45 miles per hour as hours become days. At 60 miles per hour the clanking and bouncing and rattling softens. At 80 miles per hour you stand up and stretch and enjoy the view from your perch through panoramic windowpanes. Days shift seamlessly into weeks as you crack the 100 mph mark. At 15 weeks you are approaching 150 miles per hour and there is utter silence. It is as if you are not even touching the rails. You are a flying locomotive torpedo. You press your nose up against the glass to see Canada at the 17-½ week mark, in the form of a giant, immoveable block of steel that will *stop* your locomotive dead in its tracks. The speedometer needle bounces off the brass limit dowel at 180 miles per hour as you slam into Canada at 17 ½ weeks and your locomotive comes to a violent, traumatic and sensational *stop*.

You, however, do not.

You shoot through the panoramic windshield like a bullet through a 17 ½ week long rifle barrel and skip and shred and flip and snap and tear and skid your way down the last two weeks of railroad track, finally coming to a stop at the end of the line. That last two weeks requires considerable adjustment. The train ride is an epic journey, an exploration of self that requires commitment, sacrifice, and exposing and pushing limits self imposed and otherwise. It is so great that, by comparison, the arrival, the destination, the stopping can be a bit of a train wreck. The only way I know to rid myself of that trauma is to get up, check myself for any lasting damage, and go look for another train.

"As a competitor, winner or loser, one crosses the line into limbo. The adrenaline is gone, the anticipation is gone. The verdict is either comforting or devastating but it neither returns the exhilaration of the race nor helps directly to win the next. Maybe all that matters is that there is a next."

– Stephen Kiesling – *the Shell Game*

This morning we are back on the water for an awesome row. We focus on fast hands away and slow slides, steady state at 18 strokes per minute. Rock solid, blades never touching the water, no rush, tons of ratio, absolute silence. This piece is everything that is right about rowing. It is about letting go, surrendering, trusting and getting out of your own way to achieve something greater than yourself. Then you are no longer working at it, you are invisible and a part of it. When that happens you are powerful beyond measure. I get the handshake. At the dock, Steve says, "There is an enormous investment in a pair partner." How so? "When I go out there (to the catch, specifically, and to one's limits, metaphorically) I am expecting you to be there with me." We wear perma-grins back to the boathouse.

With the oar in the other hand, I would add that there is enormous obligation and expectation in rowing with Steve. I can't go out there to Steve's limits, and that frightens me. I don't want to embarrass him or let him down. I don't want to embarrass or let myself down either. I can only explore my own limits. If I could go out there to Steve's limits, with its complicated trappings, that might frighten me for very different reasons. He expects me to be there, but can I live up to that expectation?

7. THE OARSMAN DEFINED

9/6/07: I spoke with Fritz yesterday for about 45 minutes. He is now in his forty-second year of testing U.S. National team and Olympic athletes. VO2 Max refers to the maximum volume of oxygen, measured in milliliters; a person can take up in one minute of work. For all of you fellow geeks, the formula is milliliters of oxygen per kilogram of body weight per minute. At this year's Head of the Charles he will be testing athletes from the 1972 men's eight. His research shows that these men still possess some of the highest VO2 Max numbers ever recorded, even though our VO2 Max supposedly declines about 1% per year from age 40 to 60. That decline, supposedly, doubles after age 60. These world champions, now in their 60's, are rebelling against the dogma of decrepitude. Their bodies are not doing as they are supposed to.

Yesterday afternoon Steve and I were trying to figure out how to get back to the Head of the Charles, even though our Bulldog Rowing 4+ was not prequalified this year, and we had missed the lottery cut off by exactly one month. Basically we were screwed. So imagine the cosmic serendipity when Steve informs me today that we have been invited to row for Kent Mitchell in the Men's 8+ in Boston! Oh yeah! This is huge!

The Kent Mitchell Rowing Club is one of the grand poobah mac daddies of the rolodex crews. Rumor has it that Kent, himself an

Olympian, has in his possession the most comprehensive rolodex of them all. He sits in his penthouse on the 139th floor (he is a coxswain, after all, and would not want to be over 140) of the Jamco corporate headquarters, high above the riffraff. The steel double doors to his lair reflect the flames of a giant gas fireplace as you enter beneath the gaze of genetically engineered, 6'8" doormen named Ahrens #5 and Pinsent #7. On a rug at the base of the fire, next to a heaping pile of riggers, Neapolitan Mastiffs chew on the bones of the vanquished. On his desk, next to the crystal ball that flashes worldrowing.com ticker-tape style, sits *The Rolodex*. Inside that round file spin the names, addresses, cell phone numbers, and Lear jet flight schedules of the greatest names in rowing. When Mitchell puts out the call, somewhere in that chosen oarsman's den a red light warms silently. The oarsman puts down his reading glasses, takes a thoughtful sip of brandy and excuses himself from present company. Then it's off to the secret sliding bookshelf to don trou and slide down the pole, 'cause that's what you do, covertly catching a flight to Lucerne, or Zagreb, or Green Lake. I could go on, but I might be tempted to embellish, and this is a factual account.

9/7/07: This morning we row the pair at 12 strokes per minute, blades off the water, big reach, long and silent and balanced and seemingly infinite. 12 strokes per minute. One stroke every 5 seconds. At 12 strokes per minute we are masters of the universe. It hurts to stop. To stop is to induce the pain of longing. It breaks my heart to stop. This is a whole new place we have gone to. As Jim Dietz said, this is uncharted territory. The pursuit of excellence is terrifying and thrilling at the same time.

9/9/07: Rowed a 5,000 meter head race in the pair this morning, which included a 180-degree turn as well as a giant sweeping turn. This was designed, with malice no doubt, by our friends in the mixed 8+, Diane Green and Jen Stoke. Our pair has no rudder. Pairs aren't really good for this kind of stuff. In fact, this is a stupid idea, which is precisely why we did it. Not knowing what to expect, we decided that it was of paramount importance to not take this thing seriously. In this informal Sunday event there were all kinds of boats — singles, doubles, quads, fours, eights and us… in a pair. In a head race you are not really racing each other, as it is a staggered start. You are really racing the clock. We start dead last; I think the idea being that we could do the least amount of damage to equipment and people from way back there. There is probably more than a bit of truth to that, as the pair is a comparatively slow boat and we have no rudder. We row it at about 31 strokes per minute. While it is no walk in the park, there are some good moments where we get "into the swing of things" (I wonder if that saying has its origins in rowing?). We are both surprised to find out from Jen that we have posted the fastest time of the morning. In a pair. With no rudder.

9/12/07: Started back into the hypertrophy/symmetry phase of strength training yesterday. My legs are sore today. I actually love that feeling. As I hobble up the street with my bagel, milk and coffee at 7:30 a.m. (second meal of the day, first was at 4:45 a.m.) I have a refreshing epiphany: Training is fun. My life is fun. I have the privilege of getting to use my body and mind together as a tool and a medium of self-expression. We all do! How cool is that? I think of the current crop of collegiate athletes out there and hope that they truly appreciate, every moment, in the moment, the opportunity they have before them. It should not take, as in Tammy's case, the threat of cancer to make you realize that with all that you have invested in this sport, this life, you want to be there, present, in the moment, for every stroke; for every breath. Find the love. Take big, giant strokes.

9/14/07: In the third YouTube segment, Steve's narrative mentions that we rowed at 12 strokes per minute. Carl says that he would love to see that on film. So this morning we go out with the intention of replicating that feat. There is a cloud blanket insulating us from sound and sky, the first of the fall season. The lake has dropped considerably in the last few weeks. We row in a half-full bowl, the high walls sheltering us from any wind, although there is none this morning.

The idea is to begin the workout in the 16 to 18 spm range. Then, as we get comfortable with the idea, work our way back down to 12. Steve quietly gives the call, "Ready all, row." We start, 13 spm without even thinking about it. Then 12, 11, 10… and then we disappear. Gone. The void is quiet. The void is very quiet, and bursting with energy and intensity. It is mentally exhausting to be in the void, and worth every second, every eye blink, every drop of sweat, every breath. It is not unlike the *Lord of the Rings* character that has the ring. If he wears the ring he becomes enlightened to the point of invisibility but exposes himself to his demons.

The StrokeCoach monitor will only register down to 10 strokes per minute. We are at 9 or lower, off the radar. The monitor goes blank. In the eyes of technology, we are invisible. I never knew this before because I never knew I could row a pair at 9 strokes per minute before. Up until one week ago I didn't know I could row a pair at 12 strokes per minute. In the course of just five months we have expanded and pushed the boundaries of *what if* to the breaking point of changing *what is*. The question before us is no longer what is possible but, rather, what isn't. We have systematically orchestrated a change in our reality and that is a very emotional and powerful feeling. Not to mention the fact that I have just referenced the *Lord of the Rings* and taken my level of geekiness to pantheon status. Now there really is no turning back.

9/24/07: Oh, the drama. Things have been uncertain surrounding Boston. As Kent Mitchell continues to juggle lineups, our seats are by no means guaranteed. One thing will be certain — that will be a fast boat. Meanwhile, the Bulldog 4+ has miraculously become available, although seeded in twelfth place. This can basically be recounted in the email exchange between Steve and Kent Mitchell's James Baker:

```
Steve,
     This is James Baker from Kent Mitchell
Rowing Club. You and I rowed together (with Andy
Baxter, I believe) at Canadian Masters a few years
back and have run into each other at more recent
regattas (I think the last was FISA Masters a year
ago). We are putting together a very competitive
Masters 8+ for the HOCR this October. We finished
seventh last year, having to row through a bunch
of crews as our starting position was 20th. We
hope to improve upon that result and vie for a
medal. We are looking at rounding out the lineup
and are wondering if you and Andy are interested.

Here are the other guys who would be in the crew:


CHRIS SWAN
Harvard heavy `90, Olympic spare in `92 and `96,
still training very actively, lots of masters medals.
```

JAMES BAKER
Harvard ltwt '90, US Ltwt Nat team, still training
very actively, lots of masters medals.

KIERAN CLIFFORD
Irish Ltwt Nat team, still training very actively,
lots of masters medals.

MIKE MCGINTY
Temple '91, still training very actively,
lots of masters medals.

We are also looking at several other rowers who
have national team experience from the 90's.

By the way, in doing the web search on your
name, I "discovered" that you are training for
the Olympic trials next year. That's terrific.
As someone who turns 40 in December and have
thought about a "comeback", I love the
inspiration. Hope to hear from you soon.
Regards, James

James,

Thanks! This sounds like good fun. Andy is
checking to see if he can get out of another
commitment. Should know in a day or so. We're hard
at it. Won five out of five events at this year's
Canadian Masters. One A pair beat us after a boat-
stopping crab, but we should have held 'em off.

Course the 2008 trials will be a bit tougher so we
may have to saw their shells in half (like the old
days of professional sculling...)

I'm sure Dave Potter (Yale '80) would be
up for it. He's another old-timer like me but was
2nd in the 4- trials in '80. Rows either side.
He stroked our boats at FISA. He's an awesome
stroke for a head race. Also be great at 2 or
bow. He lives in Concord MA so it's easy.
Best, Steve

Steve,

Thanks for getting back to us so quickly and
glad to hear you guys are interested. Kieran is
pulling together all the pieces so we should know
who all is in the mix pretty soon. Regarding Andy,
if his other commitment prevents his ability to go
to the HOCR, we would still be interested in your
availability.

When Kieran is figuring out boat age
averages, he'll see if bringing in Dave Potter
would let us bring in some early-30-year-old studs
of recent Nat Team experience. That might make it
all worth it. Cheers, James

James,

Andy's clear so we're in if you'll
have us.

I'm 48 — 12/4/58. Racing age is 49
Andy is 40 — 1/11/67. Racing age 41

Dave Potter is 49 12/7/57. Racing age 50 (ouch!) I haven't talked to him yet. I'll make sure he is available. Best, Steve

Steve,

Great to hear. I have to defer to Kieran now as he pulls together all the pieces. But let us know when you do talk to Dave if he is available.

By the way, I think your racing age for the HOCR is 48 years old since they do things differently than USRowing and FISA. The HOCR takes your age on race day. I know this because I was born on 12/12 so I have the same issue as you.

Also, can you confirm that Andy was born in 1967? If he was, then I think that makes his rowing age 40 years old (same year I was born). James

James and Kieran,

There's a Bulldog 4 that I've rowed in the past that has an entry. If we're not rowing with you guys, I need to get on that.

Could you let us know?
Thanks, Steve

Steve,

As far as I am concerned, you are. But Kieran is the one pulling all the pieces together. I know Kieran is juggling some average boat age issues. I'll get on him about this (I've been traveling the past week so I have not talked to him much to get the latest).

In terms of lobbying, any sense of what kind of 2k or 6k that you and Andy would pull?

James,

Thanks. This sounds like a heck of a boat. When we beat Kieran (and McGinty) in the pair with a handicap, I weighed 245 and now I weigh 220, and I'm a heck of a lot stronger. We beat all the A's in Canada except for one, and that's because we had a crab. My plan is to pull 6:00 by Feb. Not sure if I'll make it, but that's the plan. About 6:10 now. Andy's is worse but that has to do more with his head in erg pieces.
Fritz Hagerman's going to be testing that weekend, so we can all drop trou and compare...
Potter's available if we need another old guy.
Steve,

You stud. I'll pass along the details to Kieran.

By the way, I've been telling my Harvard teammates from back in the day (late 80s and early 90s) about your quest and they are all very impressed, supportive, and psyched. To quote one of them: "Kiesling? Olympic Trials? I love it!! The event is so technical that I bet he at least makes the six-man final." James

James,

Alas, Andy and I are going to bow out.
Turns out the Bulldog 4+ had our names on it,
so we're going to do that. Thanks so much for
thinking of us. My guess is you have an awesome
pool to draw from, so I'm glad we won't be racing
in the same event.
See you in Boston. Thanks again, Steve

Steve,

Sorry to hear that, but I completely
understand. And I am sorry for the long delay in
getting the lineup set, if that had any impact on
your decision. I have been trying to get Kieran to
finalize the lineup, but he has been working on
getting some Irish guys he knows to put their hats
in or opt out.

Please tell Andy that I regret that you
guys won't be powering the engine room in our
boat. I hope we have another opportunity to race
together in 2008.

Good luck in the four and I will look out
for you guys in Boston. James

James,

Re: Is the boat set? Thanks. I was best man in
Potter's wedding and haven't seen him in too long,
so I couldn't bail when we got the four...
And now he may have to be in Taiwan. So ...
if he bails and the Irish guys bail, Andy and I

would be more than happy to crawl back for seats.
We also have a cox. I'm not sure what she
weighs — not much too much — and she really
knows the Charles.)

If Potter and the Irish don't bail,
we need a starboard for our four because you
snagged Brian J. Got any extras? (This is
feeling more complicated than a high school prom)

Speaking of the Irish, I rowed in Ireland
for awhile. I don't remember any of it (especially
how the Mini Cooper ended up on the front lawn)
but I think it was really fun.
See you at the races...one way or another ...
Steve

9/21/07: So now that Potter has gotten out of his Taiwan commitment we are a go for the Bulldog 4+. But we are still missing a bow man because Kent Mitchell got Olympian Brian Jamieson before we could, so Steve asked Scott Knox if he would like to join us. Apropos of the volatile and somewhat incestuous nature of rowing, we went from no possible shot at the Charles to rowing in a hotshot rolodex 8+ full of Olympians and National team athletes to a Yale 4+ with 50% Yalies and 75% Ashland Rowing Club members. Don't know whose floor I'll be sleeping on; don't care. I'd sleep on the dock to get a seat in a boat at the Charles.

The "other commitment" I had was no less than my brother's wedding. Eric and Lise had divorced and he had found true love again with his *novia*, Sharon. Of course I would have liked to have been there, shown my support, hugged, kissed, laughed, and celebrated.

Of course there was only room in my selfish world for Boston. I would miss my brother's wedding. Eric would understand. Or he would lie convincingly.

9/28/07: This morning we bailed on weight lifting in favor of water time. We took out the old Hudson Pair, which is currently starboard rigged. This means that I would stroke and Steve would be in the bow. This thing is heavy and stable — the boat, not Steve. Steve is not overly heavy in the grand scheme of things, and if he were stable I wouldn't hang out with him. It was a nice way of mixing things up, and it was neat to be back in the old Hudson. With practically no pair experience we raced that boat to a bronze medal at the 2003 U.S. Masters National Championships. That might have been a silver medal, but Steve stopped rowing when he heard the horn at the finish line, not knowing that Berkeley Johnson and Craig Webster were ahead of us. And I caught a crab on the third stroke of the start. And there was definitely a sniper on the grassy knoll shooting at us if my nerves were to be any indication. Anyway, a pair from Greater Columbus Rowing shot by us at the finish. Our very first big race and we finished in the medals and I was thrilled. That feels like it was twenty years ago, not four.

10/1/07: Still fighting a cold and a backache, the two of which are probably related. Tanya Larsen is our massage therapist at the Medford gym. In exchange for training she has been working on my third and fourth rib for a while now. My lower back pain is actually a medial glute spasm, which has a habit of clamping down on the sciatic nerve. So while the referred pain is in my lower back, my pathology is no secret — I am a giant pain in the butt.

10/3/07: Yesterday I did a series of submaximal pieces to measure blood lactate. Having done blood lactate testing for years, I have plenty of data with which to compare. This day my numbers suck. Moral of the story is this; don't test when you are a sick, backachy pain in the butt. Your numbers will suck. That is my professional interpretation. I wonder if I can get the American College of Sports Medicine to publish that.

10/4/07: Still sick, 30-minute slog, 1:55.5

10/9/07: Yet another awesome weight workout: squats, bench pulls and stomach, followed by a 20-minute cool-down erg piece. Fritz recommended that we incorporate stomach work into all of our weight workouts. This is the finishing work after the "big" movements, squat, dead lift, bench pull, and power clean.

As much as I hate the current trendy buzzwords "core stability", its benefit to the rowing stroke is irrefutable. Facing each other, we perform 50 sit-ups passing a 25-pound medicine ball between us. For the 2005, 2006 and beginning of the 2007 training years we worked under U.S. National Team strength parameters. These are Relative Strength Factors of body weight. After Canada we started our training under Olympic strength parameters. They were too heavy. To train under those parameters would set us up for failure or injury or both. Fritz tells us that we need to embrace numbers and benchmarks rather than fear them, as they tell us where and how we should be training. To train with the wrong numbers would fail to produce the appropriate physiological response. And that, my friends, would be stupid.

Of course this is a book about rowing and training so I keep going back to the real world of numbers and physiology. But the reason

I bring these strength factors up now is different. It is due in large part to a conversation I had with my sister-in-law, Lise. We were walking the back streets along the Petaluma River in California, balancing Peet's coffees and searching for the start of the Head of the Wine Country regatta.

The conversation had its roots in the idea of intrinsic versus extrinsic motivators. Studies of elite athletes have shown that intrinsic motivators tend to produce better results than extrinsic motivators. Intrinsic motivation also helps with concentration and nerves. Extrinsic motivation does a great deal to undo concentration and exacerbate nerves. What we are talking about is the journey, not the arrival; the process, not the win. Duncan Free and Drew Ginn, the Aussie pair heavily favored to win in Beijing, say they focus on the process. They also win. A lot. Nifty extra, that.

Lise asked, "But is it *really* about the process, and not the win?" I said yes, but I got her point. Ultimately, this is about whose best, right? Hardware is good – we swear by it. As stated before, there have been some ugly, uninspired wins, and there have been some otherworldly, perfectly executed and vastly more satisfying seconds, thirds and fourths. And, when everything comes together just so, there have been some inspired and beautiful wins. But an ugly win is still a win. So what is the answer?

The answer lies in taking this to the very end, to the pinnacle, to the edge, and then shining the light back for everyone else to see. The answer lies at the finish line of the Olympic final in the men's pair in Beijing, China, August 2008. Only two men, one boat, on our planet Earth will win the Olympic gold medal that day. Out of all humanity, two men, one boat. Here is an example to illustrate where I am going with this. At the 2007 World Championships in Munich, an Olympic qualifying event, Australia wins gold, New Zealand Silver, and Great

Britain bronze in the A final. Behind them are France fourth, South Africa fifth and Serbia sixth. These are the six fastest boats in the world. We know this because before the A final there were semifinals, and before that there were reps, and before that there were heats. Before that these athletes were competing in trials with their respective national teammates. Before that they were competing to get on, and then stay on, their national team. Before that they were probably seat racing to make the varsity 8 on their college team. Are you starting to see? Stay with me.

Australia wins by 5.3 seconds over New Zealand. That is open water in a world championship final. That's crazy. 13.56 seconds passes from the time Australia crosses the finish line until Serbia reaches it in sixth place. Freakin' time zone.

Rowing defines us. The process defines us. The religion and the philosophy define us. *The win does not define us.* If the win defined us, then everybody who aspired to win the world championships, including the other five boats in that A final, the other six boats in the B final, the other countries that didn't even make the final, would be failures and lead tortured lives because of it. Athletes have, in point of fact, led tortured lives, and tortured the lives of those around them, because the *win* defined them, win or lose. When they fail to attain that standard, when they "lose", they are self-imagined failures, and they are getting older by the minute. When they win, the journey is over, which they probably didn't appreciate anyway because they were focusing on the arrival. The rest of the world moves on, and they are getting older by the minute.

I am training for the Olympic trials, such that when that time comes, I can give my best possible performance. Where I finish relative to the other boats in my race is secondary. That training is as much a meditation on staying in the present, on savoring the journey, on looking inward, as anything else. If we give 110% every single stroke and execute our race plan and come in dead last, I will call that a win. If we falter at the sprint, or lose our set, or get bullied into a higher stroke rate, then how we deal with those adversities will define us.

10/17/07: I have been absolutely sidelined with the flu, so I am trying to remain calm and confident as we get ready to leave for Boston. Yesterday I did a 5,000 with a heart rate monitor on to check my recovery. I stayed between 132 and 138 beats per minute for the first 13:30 before creeping up, which is OK. Cardiac Creep, or Cardiac Drift, usually occurs about the time your sweat response kicks in. Even though the workload hasn't changed, you are now pumping plasma to both the working muscles and the surface of the skin for temperature regulation, so heart rate increases. That's the short version. In theory, the greater your aerobic base the longer you can exercise before your heart rate begins to drift.

Then Steve and I did another 5,000, which also felt fine. This morning, Wednesday, I did a 6k at which hurt more than it should have. Hmm, might still be a little weak. I'll do a light piece tomorrow, take Friday off, race Saturday and hope for the best.

Actually I'm not hoping for anything. We're going to empty the tank and leave everything on the Charles River and it's going to hurt and more importantly it's going to hurt the other guy a lot more … bring it.

8. BENCHMARK #3 – BOSTON

The Head of the Charles Regatta is a worldwide event, known as a head race, which is about 5,000 meters in length. The Charles River is a winding, serpentine monstrosity with bridges and abutments, currents and winds and other boats with which to compete for space. There are collisions with abutments and crashes with other boats, clashes of oars and all manner of threats and curses. Two years ago the Peking University men's 8+ made their United States debut at the Charles. After making seemingly innocuous contact with another boat, they later sank in the middle of the river. Unlike traditional racing where every boat has its own lane and goes off the line at the same time, a headrace is a race against the clock. There is just one lane. Either you overtake boats and suffer the pain of exceeding physiological demands, or you give way to overtaking boats and concede defeat to the pain of exceeding physiological demands. 5,000 meters is a long way. Unlike 1,000 sprint racing, the head racer must take careful inventory of how much energy is in the tank, and distribute it wisely. Too much too soon and it's all over. Too little too late and the result is the same.

It is now Thursday and I've been back since Sunday night. I should have written sooner so as not to lose the freshness of the experience, but I did not. I think that there is a certain amount of processing that needs to take place. So here we go.

I got up at 3:30 a.m. Friday morning and picked up Scott and drove to the airport. Steve met us there. We flew together to Boston via San Francisco. Dave Potter picked us up there and we immersed ourselves in Boston traffic en route to Dave's house in Concord. Dave and his wife Johanna have to be some of the nicest people in the world, and I'm not just saying that because I got lasagna, apple crisp and a place to sleep. Traditionally they have held the pre-race dinner for the Bulldog Rowing Club and let the out-of-towners invade their home and sleep wherever there was space. We eat heartily and gratefully then descend to the basement to watch some Head of the Charles tapes and crash on the floor. Life is good. Again, how did I get here? This is Steve's world and these are Steve's friends. I am infinitely richer to now know them, but I did not sweat, bleed and fight my way through the ranks at Yale to develop these bonds, this history. This is not my story. These are the characters from Steve's story, literally the characters that I read about in my collegiate youth: surreal.

Saturday morning we get coffee, fruit, and banana pecan pancakes. I threaten to move in. Their kids will be off to college soon enough, so they'll barely notice me. We drive out to the Charles River and find the Yale trailers. A person can barely move along the pathways because the crowds are so large. The final tally for the weekend was 305,000 spectators and 8,220 athletes from 17 countries. Tom the boatman, conservative with the spoken word, directs us to our boat. I am hoping for something really good. Of course Yale has excellent equipment, and in the past we have rowed perfectly good Vespoli racing shells. But for whatever reason or maybe no good reason at all, I've never been much of a Vespoli guy. Maybe it's simply because Vespoli is on the East coast so I haven't had as much exposure to them. Maybe it's an East coast/West coast thing, like Tupac and Big E Smalls, but without the rap music and gunplay.

On the West coast, most rowers cut there teeth (and hands and calves and feet) on Pocock racing shells. George Pocock's dad built boats for England's Eton College. George and his brother Dick came to the U.S. via Canada, setting up shop in Seattle in 1911. Later Dick would head east to become the boat builder for Yale. Ironically, Mike Vespoli would coach at Yale before becoming a boat builder. In 1923 the University of Washington won the National Championship in a Pocock racing shell. It was at that point that the legacies of both entities became intertwined. In college I never thought of Pocock shells as being particularly fancy, rather purpose-built and bomb proof. On the West coast at least, every rower at some point in his or her career had seat time in a beat up, creaky, decades old Pocock shell that just refused to give up the ghost.

In 2005, then the head coach for the Ashland High School crew, I rallied for the purchase of a brand new Pocock 4+. No more hand-me-down boats that had bled out their best strokes years before. Many a car wash, yard sale and matching fund later we had raised the money and placed the order. I still have the receipt as a memento of how far the program had come since Steve had created it seven years before. To "purpose-built" and "bomb proof" I can now add the adjectives "cutting edge" and "beautiful" to describe the Pocock shell; Great boat.

Tom, who must be a wise man with infinite patience to do what he does, points up. "That's yours." On the second tier of the second trailer, above a sea of Yale blue tumult, rests a brand new Hudson bowloader 4+ (A "bowloader" has the coxswain in the front of the boat, laying down feet first, facing forward). Life is very good, indeed. We both like Hudson Boat Works, a Canadian boat builder, a lot.

Steve and I take the Hudson down and rig it. We can

practically rig a Hudson with our eyes closed so it goes fast. Twenty feet away, U.S. Men's coach Mike Teti is talking to Bryan Volpenhein. I resist the urge to wade through the masses for an autograph. I'm sure that Coach Teti would acknowledge us as little more than an annoyance. Joyce Nett is our coxswain, Yale '79. I have had the privilege of rowing for Joyce at the Charles before. The Head of the Charles is known as a "coxswain's race" in that it is a highly technical and tactical race. Big turns, penalty buoys and seven bridges over the course of three miles, not to mention overtaking slower boats, showcase the coxswain's talents. But that is just the steering side of the equation. Getting the most out of the crew, pushing them to dig deeper than they ever have without breaking them or causing resentment or rebellion, crushing and demoralizing the opponent, this takes a special kind of person; part leader, part coach, part demon, part savior; strength of character that renders them utterly fearless in battle and could not possibly be confined by physical size. Rowing may be a spiritual journey, but racing is still war.

The best coxswains are inherently, fundamentally confident, which is not to say that they are mean-spirited or angry (those characteristics make for the very worst coxswains). They are natural-born leaders. They are natural-born killers. Joyce is a very good coxswain. In her words, "We leave it all out there. We take no prisoners." My first race with Joyce was in 2001. When a boat refused to give way, we passed them on the outside. As we took seats, Joyce found the weakest link and went to work, talking loud enough for the other boat to hear, "Look at bow seat. That guy looks like he's dying. Let's get around these jokers before that guy has a heart attack." Crush and demoralize. This year, as we overtake a boat, she says, "I'm done with these guys; I have no use for them anymore. We're movin' on to the next boat." If I'm pulling my guts out and a boat catches me from behind and walks through me, that's bad enough. But then to be audibly dismissed by the cox as nothing more than a marker on some larger agenda, that's psychological warfare.

We had a great race at the Charles and Joyce was brilliant. We started in ninth place and finished in fifth, guaranteeing our spot for next year, when we will run a slightly higher stroke rate of 33 to 34 with less traffic to deal with. And that will be good. Unfortunately, Fritz did not make it back to Boston this year. His wife Marge had suffered a stroke. She has since made, in Fritz's words, "a miraculous recovery."

After milling about the tents and meeting some of the National Team guys, we head off to Joe Bouscaren's house for dinner. Now Dr. Bouscaren, Joe was a teammate of Steve's at Yale, and a central character (the others being Tiff Wood, Charlie Altekruse, Brad Lewis and John Biglow) in David Halberstam's *The Amateurs*. In true collegiate fashion, with no showers, we change clothes outside Potter's car in the darkness of Bouscaren's enormous driveway. I hate dressing up, which for me means wearing anything with buttons. We make our way to the front door. I get the sinking feeling that I am entering the lion's den. Impressive even among other lions' dens, this one currently houses the supreme alphas - Harvard and Yale alumnus, National Team and Olympic oarsman, doctors and venture capitalists, and soon a lone hyena from Humboldt State. One of the wait staff hands me a glass of white wine then retreats through a swinging door to the kitchen. If I could make it to that door I could hide in the kitchen with the wait staff and my glass of wine and pick at the leftovers and – "Now who are you and what are you doing here?" A big bald Blue, or possibly a closely cropped Crimson cuts off my escape route from the kill zone. He's not wearing a jersey, so I can't tell which. I swallow hard, "andy baxter." "Speak up; it's loud as hell in here." "Andy Baxter. I am training with Steve Kiesling for the Olympic pair trials." He looks me up and down while popping another cashew into his mouth, "You and Kiesling? Is he fucking nuts?" I want to answer *why yes he is, but he's really, really strong*, but no answer is needed. I regret that the question is rhetorical. An answer would have been welcome filler to the impossibly awkward space that I now inhabit. I am sweating and I can feel my face getting red and this collar is claustrophobic and these shoes are stupid. Maybe now would be a good time to switch to red wine. Where is that waiter?

My Deux Ex Machina comes in the form of a somewhat familiar face. I don't know where Duncan Howat went to college. I don't even know if he did go to college. I know of him only by reputation, by what Coach Jim Sims has told me, and by what I have seen of him on the water over the years. Duncan and fellow tough guy Landon Carter are members of the Pisten Bully Rowing Club. They are their own rolodex crew. They rarely lose. When they do it is usually to each other.

Based on legend and hearsay, I can recount to you these facts: Well before the dawn of cage fighting and westernized mixed martial arts, Duncan Howat made his living bare-knuckle boxing grizzly bears in the coastal regions of Alaska. When it was learned that the "grizzly bear" was actually Carter wearing a throw rug, the gig was up. The two men pulled trees out of the ground (they would probably pay for that tomorrow) and got to work whittling two single sculls, oars and riggers. They then launched under cover of darkness. If I remember my facts, based on legend and hearsay, Howat headed south and Carter ended up in New Zealand.

I had a nice talk with Mr. Howat. While my race was done, his is the next morning. I asked him how he felt. He replied that he really hadn't been rowing much, so he was not sure what tomorrow's outcome would be. The next morning, 64 year old Duncan Howatt won the Veteran Men's single sculls at the Head of the Charles...again.

Jerry Cosgrove, president of the Sports Lactate Group, put me in touch with Andrew Medcalf. Andy is a coach at the Pennsylvania Athletic Club, Penn AC for short, and has agreed to share his wisdom with me, a consultant of sorts. Coincidently, this is where Steve trained with Mathew Labine, under coach Ted Nash, for the 1984 pair trials. The rowing world is a small one, and Steve's shadow looms large.

Like Jim Dietz, Andy Medcalf is also a massive breath of fresh air; a passionate student of the art of rowing and the training process. I look forward to soaking up whatever he throws my way.

We have been doing some pretty major slogs. The day before yesterday I did a 5,000 in the morning. That afternoon Steve and I did a workout that Medcalf had suggested, 10 minutes on, 1 minute off, six times. This solves Fritz's issue of quality over quantity. We both kept our heart rates below 132 bpm. Yesterday was a weights day. With no rest between movements we squat 225 lbs. ten times, leg press 600 lbs. twenty times, then wall sit for 90 seconds. Then incline dumbbell press and triceps press. Then repeat the whole thing twice more.

Upper body pushing motions don't factor heavily in rowing, and for just that reason we include some in our routines to maintain balance. Then we finish with the obligatory medicine ball sit-ups, passing the 25-pound ball back and forth while performing a full sit-up forty to fifty times, depending on what is left in the tank. Yesterday was a forty day. We figure that the previous day's 60-minute erg piece, even though broken up into 10-minute segments, is still a 60-minute erg piece, and we feel it.

11/8/07: Yesterday we went out to the boathouse to meet with John Darling, a freelance writer. The idea is that he would interview us then join Coach Joe in the launch and have his photographer take some pictures. Photo guy never showed up. As Steve and I talk, I have a grand epiphany.

My epiphany does not confirm me as enlightened. Rather, it probably shines a glaring light on how thick I am to be just getting this now, after all this time. The epiphany is this — what we are doing is *so much bigger than us*. We are just a cog on a gear that will someday be a part of some massive machine. How we finish at trials doesn't matter nearly as much as the fact that we *show up* at trials. Maybe ten years from now when "old guys" show up regularly and aren't even thought of as old guys, we can smile and say, "Wow, we helped start that!" If 50 is the new 30, what will 60 be 20 years from now? I'll let you know in 20 years.

11/14/07: Zen and the Art of the Stupid Factor. Today we meet the photographer at the boathouse. Realistically this is our only shot at this photo thing. I pull into the parking lot and am greeted by an audible howl. This is, unquestionably, a harbinger of stupidity. The Ashland Airport, four miles up the road, reports winds from the south at 25 to 30 knots. I crest the bank of the dam and look down. White caps and rollers. Big white caps and big rollers. This would be stupid in an 8+. This would test our swimming skills in a 4+. Without question, without doubt, this is unrowable in a pair.

We have to hang on tight as we carry the pair to the dock. The wind is pulling it from our grasp, using its surface area against us. Setting it into the water, the waves are coming over the windward edge of the dock. As I place my dry socked foot into the center of the boat, the first of many waves crests the port gunwale. We haven't even launched yet, and we are taking on water. The stupid factor is rising steadily.

If we can get across the lake we might find some sheltered water. We quickly determine that a straight shot is the only option we have. A small boat like a pair cannot get out of, or over, the trough of large rolling waves. Less than 10 strokes off the dock, and Steve takes a wave right in the back. It's November and the water is cold. As I thank the gods of wind and water for sparing me the same fate, I too take an icy breaker on the back. Maybe the stupid factor also goes to eleven.

Coach Joe scouts out some halfway decent water and photos get taken. Then comes the realization that we still have to get back. We untie our shoes in anticipation of not making it back above water. The idea is that, if you do flip, it can be difficult and stressful to be stuck underwater still attached to your boat. Untying ones shoes actually has a calming effect. Once you accept your fate there is much less to worry about. We make it back with about 2 inches of freeboard left, practically underwater, laughing at the world.

11/21/07: One stroke at a time. We train through the winter at decidedly low intensities and high volumes. One of the greatest risks during the winter is to turn on the autopilot switch in your head. The problem with the seemingly endless meters on the erg is that if one is not mindful and in the present, they can lead to bad habits and injuries. The key to all of this training is stay mindful and in the present; to see every stroke as an opportunity to effect change or reinforce what is already right. What a waste it would be to not take advantage of that! Indeed, how rare is that to be in a situation where you have the potential to control and master your environment?

One of the tricks to being effective at this is to break up the long workouts into smaller chunks. If I'm doing an hour piece I'm practically brain dead 30 minutes into it. By breaking it up into three times 20 minutes, six times 10 minutes, or five times 12 minutes with a minute's rest in between, I can stay focused for the duration. As Medcalf says, "Use this time to master your skills. Take one stroke at a time." It's hard to be mindful and brain dead simultaneously.

11/25/07: At this point in our training we have two precise points of focus — more reach at the catch and clean exits. When we are mindful of those two things, really cool stuff happens. Sure, I could I could be more specific, breaking down the mechanics and hydrodynamics of propulsion theory, but let's leave it at this metaphysical truism: when we are mindful and in the present, *really cool stuff happens.*

The art of reaching without reaching. As a child of the 70's, I can't forget the scene in Bruce Lee's movie "Enter the Dragon" when he is asked to describe his style. He responds with something like, "Think of it as the art of fighting without fighting." Of course when Bruce said it, it sounded more like "dee ought of fii-ing wifout fii-ing." Martial art movie references aside, when we think too much, or too hard, about something we can become our own worst enemy. We put up our own pre-set barriers, limits, and perceptions of what is. While coaching a master rower on the erg, I noticed that very bad things were happening at the catch. His back was collapsed, shoulders scrunched up around his ears and his head was pointing down toward the floor. I asked him what he was thinking of as he approached the catch. He said, "More reach." Hmmm. I infuse some pause drills, breaking the stroke down in to smaller and more palatable neuromuscular bites. With his chest up, shoulders relaxed and chin level, he now gets more reach and more oxygen with more mechanical power and less risk of a lumbar vertebra flying across the room much like what flew out of John Hurt in the movie "Alien." He is now reaching without reaching. By letting go of what he thought reaching was, and focusing instead on the mechanics of good form, the reach comes on its own.

Martial artists don't strike at an object, but through the object. Great drummers don't see the drumhead as the end point of their drumstick's path, but a point beyond. In both cases the subject has shifted their perception of reality. They are operating in a framework that we can't see, the results of which cannot be denied.

I have a piece of tape on the starboard gunwale of our pair. A host of measurements tells me that this is where my oar handle should be to achieve sufficient reach at the catch. At one time that piece of tape represented my peak, my maximum. I would, quite literally, reach for that benchmark. Now that piece of tape on the side of my boat is just a piece of tape on the side of my boat. It is something that my oar handle casually passes over as I reach through that point to some point well beyond. It is not that I am thinking about getting more reach relative to some prescribed limit. It is that I am mindful and in the present and really cool stuff is happening.

You can do it.

Carol Lee Rogers grew up cross country skiing, swimming, playing tennis and back packing in Santa Fe, New Mexico. Not running or bicycling though. Her aspiration was to compete in the Olympics in cross country skiing. Her family moved to Colorado. In 1980 she tried cycling; absolutely hated it. Later she tried running. Nothing formal, no instruction; just ran, but ran well. In 1984 she set the course record, 2:36.37, for the Imogene Pass Run. This is no small feat. This run begins in Ouray, Colorado (elevation 7810 feet) and travels 17.1 miles over the Imogene pass (13,120 feet) to Telluride (elevation 8820 feet). This year marks the 25th anniversary of her course record, which still stands.

Carol Lee thought that maybe cross training on a bicycle would improve her skiing, so she approached the bike again. She trained in the hills, acclimating to the steep mountain passes, committing to staying in the saddle and hammering the peddles versus standing up. The Peugeot racing team noticed. In 1985 she took *two* third place mountain stages in the Tour De France. In 1986, the same year that Greg Lemond won his first Tour De France, Carol Lee finished 12th overall and, for the second time, was the second fastest American.

She finished her racing career "2nd or 3rd, I can't remember" in the 1988 Coors Classic, and mountain biked throughout East Germany before moving to Ashland in 1995 - Super hero stuff, right?

In 1976 Carol Lee's almost lifeless body was found on a road in Switzerland with a massive head injury. Nobody knows what happened. After a six day coma and brain surgery, she was flown back to the states. While coping with neuromuscular re-patterning and visual spatial awareness ("wind in the trees scared the hell out of me"), her own voice spoke to her. "You can do it." She listened to her voice, "You can do it!"

Carol Lee has been with me since we opened on Hersey Street in 2004. A trainer, neural linguistic practitioner, yoga teacher and nordic walking coach, her own business is called "You Can Do It!" Not a bad gig for me, of course, to work with my heroes.

12/5/07: Yesterday was Steve's birthday. Today is his first row in his fiftieth year. It is cold, cloudy, pea soup weather and we are the only people on the lake; the entire lake to ourselves. Four 10-minute pieces at 17 to 18 strokes per minute. Upon our return, while stepping back on to the dock Steve says, "Oh shit!" Alarmed, I blurt out, "What's wrong?"

Did the oar break? Did he miss an important call or forget to pick up his kids? Is the boat OK? Did I leave my headlights on? "We are going to the Olympic trials," he says. Well, yes … there's that.

"Our biggest fear is not that we are inadequate; our biggest fear is that we are powerful beyond measure. It is our light, not our darkness that most frightens us. We ask ourselves: 'Who am I to be brilliant, gorgeous, talented and fabulous?' Actually, who are you not to be?"

— Nelson Mandela

9. BREAKING DOWN

12/19/07: Last week we pulled the entire rig and moved it toward the bow but left the foot stretchers unchanged. This increases the catch angle but does not change our center of gravity in the boat. After two pieces we move the foot stretchers 1 notch toward the bow, which moves our center of gravity. The idea is to get the boat to level out, dropping the bow and creating a more stable platform. We can tell the difference immediately. Once we find our impeller, which we took off for Canada, we will do some tests, then continue to adjust. It's getting cold out there.

12/23/07: More of the same, 17 to 18 strokes per minute on a winter Sunday afternoon.

1/15/08: Work has been extremely busy. I opened *Baxter Fitness Solutions for Fifty and Beyond* in Ashland, Oregon on October 2004. Now, one year and three months after opening my second facility in Medford, Oregon I have a patent pending on my system and a licensing agreement in development with MedEx fitness centre in Victoria, BC. I have been investing a great deal of myself to my work, which is physically and emotionally taxing.

On January 5, Steve and I sat down with a four-month calendar to map out the rest of our training leading up to the trials. There is a new, potentially disastrous twist in the game plan. Apparently the pair trials will also be used to determine the Big Boat lineups. This means that the top six fastest pairs will determine seats for the 8+ and the 4- for the Olympics. In addition, the whole shooting match will start with a time trial. Only the top eighteen boats go through to the heats. So now we are not just racing the pair event, but have to contend with the biggest of the big boys, which could push us right out of range to even get a shot at the pair. At last year's trials there were twenty pairs in the time trial; fourteen of them were from the national team camp at Caspersen Training Center. Realistically, that meant that only four of the six "outsider" pairs would even make it through to the heats. Two pairs went home before the real racing had even begun.

1/15/08: Did a 5,000 at 23 spm, 1:51.8 split, then weights. My back had been giving me fits for a month, so it felt *great* to finally be back in the weight room. At 7:00 a.m. this morning, after a 12k recovery piece I walked to Adam's Deli on the corner. I ordered a smoked turkey and veggie bagel, a bagel with peanut butter, a fruit cup, orange juice and a coffee to go. While waiting, I decided to sit down. Curious, because in the fourteen months since we opened our second gym up the street from Adam's, I have never sat down; always stood at the counter. As I sat there, my last coherent thought was that my legs were numb … then I just fell asleep! 41 years old (my birthday was on the eleventh) and I am back in school again, where life takes on a hazy, floaty existence between training sessions.

1/16/08: Back on the water for our first interval session of the year. Rich Lavoy and Scott join us in another pair where we will be doing 25 strokes on, 20 off. Up to this point we haven't done anything over 24 spm. Steve has been sick. Because he is Steve, the only logical thing to do is kick the crap out of himself on the erg. So Monday he kicked the crap out of himself on the erg. That was bad. He was up all night with diarrhea and a fever. Now we are on the water in January doing sprint work and we've got another pair to race and coach Joe and Dan Hirsch are in the launch and Carl is filming.

After the first four pieces, which are fairly sloppy, I tell the guys that we will do only two more because Steve is sick (we end up doing three). Rich says, "I just got out of the hospital." Hmm. It seems he was having some chest pain and ended up going in for some sort of surgical procedure. Back at the boathouse Steve is white as a sheet and wants to throw up. Rich takes off his shirt, exposing a large bandage covering his chest, just over his heart. I quip that Rich is so tough he probably just had a heart transplant and now he's racing the pair the next day. Scott adds that the surgery was probably a voluntary heart transplant and says, "He's just upgrading to a bigger model." These are the types of men you want on your side in battle, whatever your battle may be. In this case, ours would be on the aquatic battlefield of Mission Bay, San Diego for the Crew Classic in April — just three weeks before the trials.

In his opening remarks to the Stanford Alpine Club film festival and exhibit in May 2000, Al Baxter said, "I offer these personal circumstances as examples of what I believe to be a larger and more generally applicable truth: that who one climbs with and how one profits from climbing associations by incorporating them in a larger life are as important in the long run as what one climbs, how one climbs or where one climbs." I believe the same to be true of rowing.

Dad met Mom through climbing. A fiercely intelligent, strong willed Stanford rock jock, Gail Allison Fleming had no intention of playing in the same sandbox as the rose-lipped maidens. Tough, pretty and smart. "Surely this could be a girl for me," Dad would recount with a teary sparkle in his eyes and a Cheshire smile to match. Mom had a placard on her desk, next to the drafting board, across from the tennis trophies – GAIL BAXTER - GIRL ARCHITECT. On the photo board in the kitchen was a quote,

"Sure Fred Astaire was a great dancer.
But remember, Ginger Rogers did everything he did,
backwards and in high heels."

The quote started out as a page torn from a magazine. Whenever it faded or was diminished by pinholes, it would be xeroxed back to life. By the time I left for college it served to remind me of one thing – Mom was a Feminist of sorts. And Mom was a badass. That's two things. Mom was a badass Feminist. There, that's one thing. I think that I include that story because she was a forward thinker and a forward doer. I like to think that she imparted some of that to me, that it is important to keep moving forward. That plays well in the row/life parallel.

1/21/08: Went to Coos Bay for the weekend to see Denise's sister and family; brought my erg in the back of my truck. I also looked at the film from last weekend. I'm dropping my right elbow at the finish again, sinking at the finish — too much time on the erg, not enough on the water. Rowed 25,000 meters today as part of Medcalf's five-week cycle of training. Currently two days a week are 25,000 meter days, two days are 17,500 meters plus weights, and two days are 15,000 meter plus water time, with one day off.

1/22/08: 10,000 meters this morning, then a 5,000 with Steve at a comfortable 1:54.1 split then squats, four times 8 at 225 lbs., deep enough to test my back. It held up fine. I notice while looking at video that Jason Read also drops his elbow at the finish. That may well be the only thing about rowing that we have in common. As thorough as our training program is and as good as I feel, every affirmation carries with it the unspoken trailer "for a 41-year-old." The trials are now on my mind daily. I get up at 4:15 a.m. instead of 4:45, as I need the extra half hour to fit in the training. But I don't dread it. I look forward to it. I love the energy of the early morning. Every workout, two to three times per day, is accounted for. I look forward to the training because it is tangible. The Olympic trials are not. Focusing on the training helps me to *not* focus on the trials; Thinking Bad, Doing Good. It occurs to me, right at this moment that this might be the biggest, baddest, scariest train ride I have ever been on. Cool!

1/23/08: Had a 60-minute piece this morning (four times 15 minutes). On the fourth piece my heart rate was higher than it should have been, and that is never a good sign. This afternoon is a water workout, and the wind is howling. Nobody is getting on the water this week because of wind; Frustrating. Sitting in the parking lot at the boathouse we share similar feelings of being weak and feeble, and absolutely loathing the erg. The water workout was supposed to be two times 2000 meter pieces, 25 strokes on at race pace, 20 strokes off. So now we are committed, at least in principle, to going in to the boathouse and doing that workout…on the erg.

I mention that a warm cup of coffee would be much nicer, or even heading back to the gym for more weights, or playing in traffic, anything but the erg. We warm up for 5 minutes and go through the obvious statements – "this is going to hurt a lot", "this is going to suck", "this is not going to be pretty", "why don't we just vomit now and get it over with", the usual stuff. The first piece is always a bit of a "testing the waters" piece. If you dive too deep into the pain tank you may not make it back out to survive the entire workout. At least that's the way I see it. I pull 1:31. Steve pulls 1:28. So it begins. We get through the first piece without any drama, none. Of course it's hard and uncomfortable, but not the kind of pain that gets down deep into what George Pocock calls "The you of you" and twists until you cringe and cower and cry for it to stop. Surely the second piece will be a fight for survival, a pain fest like so many before it. And that ... just does *not* happen. We hit it hard and in control.

The splits continue to drop. The pain is kept in check. I finish the workout at a 1:27 and Steve finishes at 1:24. In some perverse way we finish refreshed and excited. This is working!

1/24/08: 30-minute piece in the morning, then a 20k in the afternoon. That's 20,000. Twenty thousand meters. On the erg. The first 20 minutes go by with plenty of conversation and laughs. The next 20 minutes we just settle into a comfortable groove. As we hit 50 minutes I am thinking that I could do this all day. At 53 minutes I notice aches and twinges, in my rib, lower back, and hip. At 57 minutes my abs start to lock up. I am cramping up and breaking down. At 60 minutes I grab a drink of water and push through the cramps and visualize the water working its way through the muscle cell walls, altering the Ph balance within the cell and enabling the contracting fibers to release. It works. In my mind I am no longer breaking down, I am breaking through.

In my visualization (trust me, you can imagine anything after 60 minutes on the erg) I have pushed through a thin brown paper barrier into a lush meadow, not unlike any of the alpine meadows of my High Sierras youth. We reach deep into the vertical rubber frame bumper of the Concept 2 rowing machines at 23 strokes per minute, practically floating through the last 20 minutes and amassing 20,000 meters with a heart rate of 132 bpm.

1/25/08: This morning I get up a bit slow for my 5:30 a.m. erg workout. Short story is, 15 minutes into my piece my heart rate is over 140 bpm. I am obviously not recovered from yesterday so I stop. This afternoon is a 5,000 meter piece plus weights. I start where I left off last week at 1:54, increasing power every 1000 meters by 4 seconds, which felt really good. Squats, seated rows and abs and this week is *done*. Tomorrow is a day off. Steve says that we should drink heavily ... juice, milk, water, whatever we can get our hands on. I agree heartily.

1/26/08: Hung out with the kids, ate pizza and chocolate chip cookies, drank a gallon of milk and it was just grand.

1/27/08: Took the San Diego 8+ out this morning. Arghh, the sea, she was angry. Not quite white caps, but big rollers. The problem with rollers, other than their ability to roll you if caught broadside, is that your blade can hit them on the recovery. That being said we had a pretty decent row. After practice I comment that, although I didn't catch any crabs, I sure decapitated a few. The winds continue to pick up, and by 11:00 a.m. the snow is coming in sideways. I do a 10,000 meter erg piece in my garage with the doors open so I can watch the snow drifts pile up; they do at an alarming rate. The annual Ashland Rowing Club banquet, scheduled for tonight, is cancelled due to snow.

The U.S. Olympic Committee requires that I fill out a form

entitled "athlete autobiographical information." It has the usual stuff, like height and weight, where you went to college, what your degree is and so on. As I make my way down the list I fill in the "high school" space followed by the "year graduated" space. I type in '85. The U.S. Olympic Committee Athlete Autobiographical Information form tells me that the year I have entered is invalid. I try "1985." I am again told, in no uncertain terms, that the year I have entered is invalid. There was that time I wore a dress to school to challenge the dress code. Or the time I concocted and drank a roast beef and beer milkshake, but that's hardly cause to invalidate a whole year. Perhaps this has something to do with the fact that, for others filling out the U.S. Olympic Committee Athlete Autobiographical Information form, 1985 would be the year entered under Date of Birth.

The U.S. Olympic Committee Athlete Autobiographical Information form asks me who my heroes are. I type in "me, because my children deserve one." And they do. Every kid does. Every child should see their parents as their heroes, as I did mine. Every parent should be a hero to his or her child. It is symbiotically empowering. What's your super power?

1/30/08: Finally back on the water on a no-wind day. Light snow, water like glass, air perfectly still, and mountains, blanketed in white, surround us. So we go and ruin it with interval work. Hard, race pace stuff. On the final piece a bald eagle flies behind us. This is good. Good because it is time to start getting reacquainted with speed work, with real numbers that tell us how fast we are moving the boat, and good because if we hadn't shown up we wouldn't have seen the really cool bird.

1/31/08: This morning is a 30-minute recovery piece and my left shoulder is agitated. This afternoon we do a 60-minute piece.

2/1/08: Tanya, our massage therapist, informs me that my infraspinatus is not just agitated it is downright pissed off. Getting old and training for the Olympics is apparently not for sissies. Shoulder is hot, hurts to the touch.

2/3/08: More intervals on the water this morning. It is snowing heavily enough that everything is extremely quiet, even muffled. At 35 to 36 spm we are working too hard to make the boat move well. We are working *at* rowing, not *on* rowing. At 37 to 38, everything gets light, we flow and the boat *moves*. I think that efficiency happens at the highest intensities out of necessity; otherwise the only other choice is to fall apart. This philosophy can be applied to the aging body as well. As we age we tend to shy away from high intensity work, because it is uncomfortable and because we are conditioned to believe that we will hurt ourselves because we are not twenty anymore. The medical community has not helped matters. Only two generations ago it was not uncommon to be prescribed bed rest if you had arthritis. What we now know is that if you don't provide sufficient stimulus to the working muscle you will not produce the appropriate physiological response. Fritz published a study on strength training in the senior population that proves high intensity strength training reverses the aging process at the cellular level. Others, like the Keiser Institute on Aging and Dr Walter Bortz have documented the same. Preservation of muscle mass may be the single most significant factor in our quest to maintain function and independence, because it affects so many other factors; joint support, balance, fall prevention, functional strength, metabolism, insulin sensitivity, venous support and on and on.

Dr. Robert Sallis is the president of the American College of Sports Medicine. In partnership with the American Medical Association, his "Exercise is Medicine" initiative states, "If there was a drug that had the kinds of benefits to patients that exercise does, I think that every doctor would be prescribing it and our healthcare system would see to it that every patient had access to it."

2/6/08: While so much of this is critical, objective, hard numbers stuff, the softer, subjective, psychological side of training for the Olympics in midlife warrants obvious consideration. Over the last couple of weeks Steve and I have had some pretty intense workouts in the weight room, on the ergs, and on the water. What has been so rewarding about this particular phase is that we have been the masters of our universe. We know the numbers we need to hit and we have hit them. In our discussions about why this has been so successful, these responses have arisen; my metaphor is that of taming a giant dragon. One method is to ride the dragon with unshakeable confidence, sitting calmly but assuredly at the base of his neck, taking in the view. The other is to be hanging on to the end of his tail while being tossed about wildly, hoping that you will hold on long enough for him to fatigue and come to a stop before killing you in the process; same trip, dramatically different ride. Steve puts it this way, "Either you own 'it', or 'it' owns you." Your demons are lurking down there. It can be a terrifying place. I think, sometimes, the *fear* of pain, the *fear* of failure, is more painful than the pain itself. When you overcome that fear, when you dive headfirst into that dark place and come out on the other side still alive, no, more alive, you are the master of your universe, powerful beyond measure.

Rather than bask in that enlightened state as we mortals would, the Olympian will stay down there, relishing, thriving, and feeding on that dark place and all that comes with it. The Olympian will dive deeper still, actively seeking out demons in the harder to reach crevices and crags to become the aggressor; the shark. And maybe that is the real difference between Steve and me – while some use athletics as a vehicle for facing their demons, the Olympian has found a suitable venue for realizing a darker truth. Perhaps he is the demon.

2/10/08: Rowed the San Diego 8+ this Sunday morning, 26 degrees and, thankfully, no wind chill to speak of. In the afternoon I do a 30-minute piece. This evening as I wash the dishes my blistered hands sting under the water. Blisters are normal, but my hands are swollen as well. I guess 26 degrees is cold enough.

2/11/08: Sore throat setting in, feeling tired. Went to the Ashland Rowing Club banquet, which was great but my cold is setting in fast. Man, I hate being sick.

2/12/08: Today is shot. I am sick. Spoke with Volker Nolte today. He says, with Hagerman-like (or maybe it's just Nolte-like) forcefulness, that our oars, at 370 cm, are too long given the Fat Smoothie blade design. He suggests cutting to 367 cm and working down from there. Sounds great to me, as these monsters feel heavy. The rig is starting to feel heavy now that we are maxed all the way to bow. Scott at Hudson Boat Works suggests that we go back to setting the rig such that the pin (oarlock) is perpendicular to the aft edge of the bulkhead. Translation: we are too far forward. Tiny boat feel heavy, tiny boat go slow.

2/13/08: Too windy to row, still sick. I go out to the boathouse to change the rig and the oars.

2/18/08: Well, there went a week due to sickness. *That sucks.* We seem to be developing a minute amount of national attention as to our quest. NBC Sports, among others, has picked up the Medford Mail Tribune story, *Geezers go for the Gold.* Now there are bloggers and chat rooms where folks can weigh in with their opinions as to whether or not we have a shot. From the greatest minds in the world of rowing, or at least the most vocal, we now know this: our quest is possible, though not probable, and Steve needs a haircut.

Pain, suffering, steering, and excuses. Had a great talk with Andy Medcalf yesterday morning. We are now ten weeks from the trials. This represents a major shift in our training. Now when we go to the water we go as to battle. We battle ourselves, the clock, the dragon demons and anyone else who cares to show up. Two times 2000-meter race pieces and three times 7-minute rate-shift pieces will now make up most of our limited water time. As Medcalf says, "There'll be pain, suffering, some sucking wind, maybe your steering will be off or the weather won't be right ... there will be plenty of room for excuses, but you're gonna do it. It'll take three or four weeks to adapt." Ten weeks left. We have been riding this train, sometimes perched at the controls, sometimes dangling from the caboose, for forty-three weeks. Our train is about to hit its top gear and Princeton is fast approaching.

Steve was a no-show for yesterday's afternoon workout. This happens. I had been sick and we have both been busy with things other than training, so no big deal. After my morning workout I call him to confirm our 2 p.m. training session. He answers his cell phone and says that he won't be able to make it. "Okay," I say. "I'll just see you on the water Wednesday." He says, "No, I won't be able to make that one, either." Hmmm. "Where are you?" After all, this is it. This is seriously go time. Our dragon waits. It is time for battle. Steve says, "Where am I? Well … I'm … in Maui, but I have an erg."

10. BREAKING THROUGH

2/21/08: Blisters on top of blisters, sore, creaky, stiff. And yet, I get back on the erg, again and again, and again and again. We are so hardwired to row that everything else seems almost unnatural by comparison. Steve is back from Maui as I write this and we are supposed to be on the water in two hours. The problem is that a storm is blowing in and currently winds at the lake are gusting at 22 mph.

2/22/08: Blisters under blisters, and I've developed a hot spot on my right heel. We could not get on the water yesterday, but stayed at the boathouse and did an hour piece. Steve had gone to Maui in pursuit of a girl. We spent the hour talking about blisters, Obama, Clinton, and why the Olympic trial was a fate worse than death. Typically you don't systematically beat the crap out of yourself in preparation for death. Both will be painful, but one is avoidable. When you die, presumably you go to a better place. When you finish the Olympic trial, win or lose, you're still in New Jersey.

2/24/08: Rowed the San Diego 8+ this morning in truly crappy conditions. Three times 7-minute pieces with rate shifts. Above 30 spm it just kind of fell apart. But that is where that boat is right now, working the kinks out.

My nine-year-old son Garrett is coming home from a field trip to the Oregon Caves. At 8:00 p.m. I stand in the parking lot at Bellview Elementary school, waiting for the bus full o' kids with all of the other parents. I live a pretty isolated and insulated life in many ways. I'm a rower, for one thing. That particular kind of fanaticism is best understood by other rowers, possibly only understood by other rowers. When I'm not rowing or training for rowing I practically live in a gym. I spend most of my waking hours in environments that I have almost complete control over. I am in my element, so to speak. So when I leave the comforts of my self-realized universe, I sometimes feel like an alien. I feel like a rower out of water. I look at what's going on around me and I don't get it. I look at people around me and I think that they don't get it. My reality is not their reality and their reality is not my... "So, Garrett tells us that you're going to the Olympics." What's that? Who are you? Oh right. It's 8:00 p.m. and I'm in the parking lot at my son's school waiting for his bus. Field trip. Caves. Rain. Other parents. "Well, I'm training for the Olympic trials." Other parents stop their idle chitchat and try not to stare. Or they just stare anyway.

In the world of comedy timing is everything. My world is a pretty funny one, so I'm a big fan of timing. This father of a nine year old has unwittingly stepped in to my world, where I am the master of my universe. So now I have control over everything and can see what will happen next. With Johnny Carson like precision, I slowly and subtly pull back the imaginary golf club. It's really not much of a zinger, but it is so obvious to me what is about to happen that I just have to play it. Timing is everything. The imaginary golf club descends in a gentle arc. I make a soft "tock" sound with my tongue. As I make contact with the imaginary ball he says, "Aren't you kind of *old* to be doing that?" Zing! I hold my hand, visor like, at my brow, watching my shot trail off into the darkness. Eyes fixed on the trees I reply, "Yeah, well, that's kind of the point…"

2/26/08: I reread that previous bit about the trials. I realize that it is not nice to be a smart ass just for the sake of humor at the expense of someone, or something, else. The Princeton, New Jersey area is actually quite stunning.

We are at our highest training volume to date — 11.5 hours this week. That is roughly 30,000 meters per day, with Saturday off. That is ergs and weights and water time. That is planning meals between clients while working eleven hours a day running two facilities. That is doing homework and piano with my son and refereeing play dates with my now 6-year-old daughter. That is being supportive of my wife as she changes the world through her art center and that is picking up meds for my mother-in-law who is living with us post–knee replacement. And what does all of that mean? I think it means that *life* is Olympic. It is not that any of *that* is bad or that any of *that* is good. It is just that *that is.* Tomorrow we will do the first two times 2000-meter races in the pair, wind permitting. Squats this afternoon feel weak and painful.

2/27/08: I heard from a family friend that Sebastian Bea, 2000 Olympic silver medalist in the pair, got a pay raise and a six-month leave of absence to train full time at Princeton for the trials. Good for him for creating that. I am lucky if I get 5 minutes long distance per two weeks with Andy Medcalf to discuss our training. Waaa, waaa, waaa. Not that I am so delusional as to compare myself to Sebastian Bea. I think I might be stressing just a *little bit* over these 2k's. Ya think?

2/28/08: It is with great relief that I report the completion of our first set of 2K races on the water. Not that they were any good. The steering sucked, the weather sucked with rollers and wind, and we generally sucked wind, but they are done! It was everything coach Medcalf said it would be.

First of all we put the rudder back on and we just do not do well with that thing so we disconnected it for the second piece. We rowed a course that was essentially a mirror opposite image of San Diego's Mission Bay. Starting from a protected cove we are blasted with wind and rollers off the starboard bow at the 500-meter mark. At 1000 meters we find our groove and regain our boat speed only to get blasted again for the last 500 (that does not happen in San Diego unless you're stuck out in lane 6, in which case the entire universe is out to get you anyway, so why not throw a little extra wind into the cosmic soup bowl?).

What is great about these terrible pieces is that, given all of the external stuff, the wheels did not come off. We did not fall apart. Yes the times sucked and the rowing sucked and it is clear that we desperately need more water time after being on ergs all winter, but internally, emotionally, we still owned it. And I am going to have to go on record as saying that this is quite an accomplishment. We have eight weeks left in which to take all of this training and turn it in to some kind of boat speed.

2/29/08: Leap day. How fitting that we are leaping into the final phase of our training. Steve feels that we need to back off on the volume as we focus on high-intensity race-pace training. First and foremost we do have to listen to our bodies. We took yesterday off completely, then this morning I did a nice 30-minute piece at 1:57 just to get the blood flowing and it felt great.

Every year, year in and year out, the March-April training cycle means two things to me. It means more water time leading to the beginning of racing season, and it means more discord at home. When I am in race mode, I am not there for my family. Obviously I am traveling more, so I am away from home a lot. But what really causes problems is that I am not "there", not present and actively participating in the goings on around me. I am consumed and myopic. I am aloof.

3/1/08: Today we race a 2000 meter piece against a women's quad and a double. With no real warm-up to speak of and then just crushing the first 500 meters, we are quickly in the pain tank and everything comes unglued. The last time I endured that kind of pain was at the World Masters Games in Edmonton, Canada, 2005. Our trailer had flipped, smashing up a bunch of our shells. Boats were in short supply as there was a trucking strike and the western seaboard looked like a parking lot for shipping containers. It was already pretty ugly by the time the Russians were caught stealing a boat from the storage yard and trying to hide it in the bushes. We managed to get our hands on a lightweight 4+. We weighed it down such that, with every stroke, the stern deck went completely under water. It was heavy. It was like rowing a dump truck. Today was a dump truck row.

The bad luck of the Irish – There is one race that stands out above all other races as the embodiment of pain and fear for me, and possibly for Steve too. May 6, 2006 was the Gold Rush Regatta in Sacramento, California. The information at the time was that we would be racing former National team member and Olympian Mike Still and his pair partner Craig Webster. Having rowed with Mike (in Canada for Kent Mitchell) and against Craig (in Sacramento for Masters

Nationals), Steve and I both knew that this was a lethal combination, the likes of which we had certainly never come up against. The pit in my stomach started to form easily two weeks before the race. There is racing, and then there is racing the pair. I just can't say it any other way. They are on different planes. Getting back to the microscope metaphor, there is no hiding in the pair. There is only the truth – painful, raw, and unforgiving. By the time we hit the road for Sacramento I am a complete wreck. Unlike anything before, when Steve's confidence would have shielded me from the truth, this time Steve is a complete wreck also.

Sighing and yawning are evolution's way of preparing the human body for fight or flight. They bring in extra oxygen and release nervous energy. Somewhere along the evolutionary train tracks mankind added expletives to the ritual. One hundred or so miles into our road trip the decision *between* fight and flight still has not been firmly cemented. This can best be illustrated through a series of yawns, sighs, and expletives, like so, "huuuuuuu#$%^&* I can't believe we are doing this!" That was the sigh. Now let's take a look at the yawn, "Yeeaaaaaw*&^% we could just bail and say we got a flat tire!" I imagine prehistoric man staring down the saber-toothed tiger and sighing, "huuuuuuu$%^&* Thag not that hungry. Thag prefer leafy green salad today."

When we get to the CSUS aquatic center it is hot - Sacramento hot. Walking along the footpath, trying to breathe and not shout expletives, we come upon Mike Still. He is lying under a canopy, cap pulled over his eyes, about as relaxed as any person could possibly be short of sedation. I say, "You know, this would be a perfectly good day if we didn't have to race you guys." Mike looks up. He is smiling. It is the smile of someone who knows something that we don't. "You're not racing us," his smile gets wider, teeth flashing, "You're racing those guys." Those guys are Kieran Clifford and Mike McGinty, part of the next wave of Kent Mitchell oarsmen. Clifford was an Irish National team rower and McGinty sounds Irish, so we assume he was too. You know what happens when you assume, don't you? You're stupid.

Actually, all I now know about Mike Mcginty is that he rowed at Temple University and is a Kent Mitchell regular. As far as I am concerned, at this time, they are both Olympic gold medalists and we are about to get the crap kicked out of us. Like so many other races, I don't remember who else is in that event. This is destined to be a two boat race. This is also destined to be a painful crushfest and I am scared to death.

There are different types of pain and fear. The dump truck row in Edmonton hurt because we were worn down from successive races. And we were rowing in the wrong size boat. We were far too tired to be scared of anything. That was the pain of progressive overload. That was absolutely nothing like what we were about to do.

Now we are fresh and agitated. We have been training hard. This will be a test against a young, fast, experienced pair. Now we will call on our bodies to dig deeper than maybe we ever have, one time all out, and there will be no excuses. We do this willingly, knowing that it is going to hurt. I remember looking to coach Joe for advice, possibly sympathy. His response comes quickly, "This is what you asked for. You didn't come here to race pushovers." We came, ostensibly, in pursuit of the truth, just maybe not this much truth.

At the starting line I am nauseous and dizzy. Breathing seems to be a conscious effort; as if I didn't think about it my breathing would stop. We go off the line with a three second handicap against the young Irishmen. Others have gone off the line well before us on handicap. They don't matter. By the 500-meter mark all will have been caught and passed. What matters is the pair of Clifford and McGinty. Steve and I both thought they would have caught us by the 500. Three seconds is not that much over 500 meters for guys like this. At the 500 we take our "power 20." The Irishmen have shifted as well. What we now know is that there will be no settle from the power 20. They are charging hard, building speed and momentum and probably a bit of fury. What are these old guys doing out front? Twenty strokes after the 500-meter mark and we are basically sprinting to hold them off.

If they had caught us earlier I probably would have let them go. I never expected to beat them anyway. Now with less than 200 meters to go fear and pain are accompanied by desperation and panic. We are so deep into this thing there is no way out. If the first 500 meters had played out differently we might be coasting to an easy Silver medal right now, and that would be a dramatically different reality from what is evolving. Directly in front of the spectator beach, with our club cheering us on, the microscope exposes us for exactly what we are. We are in a fight for our lives. We are pulling as hard as we can and they are coming and I don't know that we can hold them off. Nietzsche's demon must be propelling our vessel because I am numb. I can't hear. My legs don't seem to be attached to my body anymore. I look over my shoulder at the finish line. My body has stopped listening to me so I beg the finish line to come to us. I will it to come to us. The finish line takes pity and obliges. We cross the line twelve hundredths of one second ahead of the Kent Mitchell pair.

On the drive home Steve says, "It's a good thing we won that race because it would have **sucked** to work that hard to come in second." I owe those guys a beer for the hardest race of my life. I will buy them two beers if they promise that we never have to do that again.

3/2/08: The San Diego 8+ is starting to shape up nicely. Big boats can't be rushed, and motley crew's like this need to be cultivated. We had been a little rough up to this point, just trying to get a consistent lineup to train. Steve and I have been completely consumed with our training, so it is refreshing to switch gears and devote our energy to a greater cause, cogs in a bigger wheel.

3/3/08: We are back in the pair this Monday morning, trying to get a handle on how to apply our power effectively. Historically we have been a crushing crew, meaning we usually best our opponents with brutal starts that launch us out in front. In 1000-meter racing this is extremely effective. Then, if there is anyone around at the 500 mark, we take a power 20. That move is what we call the "Crush and Demoralize Move." This type of racing does not work for 2000-meter races. If you attack the first 500 too hard and stay anaerobic too long, you dive too deep into the pain tank to recover. By the time that happens it's too late. You might as well take your dump truck and go home. Our goal is to practice *not* rowing too fast, getting comfortable with a specific split and sustaining it. Steve is reticent to embrace this type of training. He is from an era where, under Tony Johnson and others, you simply attack all of the time.

As we are coming up from the dock, bickering as old married couples do, women from the recreational group, the Greens, are carrying oars down. Our club has different levels, from juniors and individuals to recreational rowers and women's and men's racing teams. Some follow our Olympic quest with great interest. They tell us that it is inspirational. Others, I am sure, see it as more of a curiosity. Others, still, don't see it at all.

I don't remember what we were arguing about. But I do remember having the impression that we made the Greens uncomfortable. So after we pass them I turn to Steve and say, in an overly loud and bickery way, "And another thing, I never liked your eggs!" With athletic comedic prowess, he volleys back, "Yeh, well you snore!" Levity reestablished, we continue up the hill toward the boathouse.

3/5/08: Too windy to get on the water this morning, so we went to breakfast instead. We *have* to get more water time. This afternoon we will do 500-meter intervals on the erg. This will be a repeat of our June workout, so we can compare numbers and see if we have made any gains or at least staved off any losses in nine months. Nine months? We officially jumped in to this thing eleven months ago, although we had been talking about it and training toward it for longer than that. I remember that workout well. 500 meters on, three minutes off. Now we go. Basically two seconds faster per piece than June. That is potentially eight seconds over 2000 meters.

3/7/08: 30 degrees this morning but, thankfully, no wind. We do 50-stroke pieces with Scott and Eric in the double. Our goal is to have complete control at a 1:45 split, rather than hammering it and tanking. Minus some steering issues we put down some really good pieces. With race starts we progress with a sequence of 5-10-35. This means a five stroke race start, ten high strokes, then settle for 35 strokes. Because the 1:45 split is now a constant, we can get a feel for how to manipulate the variables of rate and ratio relative to our current gearing. This is starting to come together really well. If I can just get Steve to believe that.

This morning's pieces are on the mark. Steve mentions that it is great to have Scott and Eric right there next to us, as it forces us to focus on the task at hand and practice relaxing under pressure.

Buddha and Lao Tzu should have rowed the pair. Buddha should probably have stroked. By the fourth piece, when things might otherwise start falling apart, we are surrendering to it, embracing it, owning it. We are going faster.

Before heading in we make some minor footstretcher adjustments and then take a 20-stroke piece to check our line. I usually glance over Steve's shoulder toward the end of a piece to see our split. As long as we finish each piece in the 1:44 to 1:46 split range on the 50-stroke pieces I know we are successful. The 20-stroke piece feels relaxed and I see that we are pulling 1:40 comfortably.

In the parking lot Steve pulls up, rolls down his window, and says, "You know we were really flying on that last piece." I don't think that 1:40 for 20 strokes is anything special. Steve is also quite conservative in his allocation of praise, so I am curious as to what would prompt him to stop his truck and push the window-down button.

"You mean that 20-stroke piece?" I ask.

"No, the last 50-stroke piece we were between a 1:30 and a 1:33. We were flying." Wow. We were flying but it didn't feel any more difficult than the other pieces. Letting go takes practice. When you let go, you fly.

"Two such as you with such a master speed
    Cannot be parted nor be swept away
    From one another once you are agreed
    That life is only life forevermore
    Together wing to wing and oar to oar."

— Robert Frost

149

A coach once said that he could teach 90% of rowing in ten minutes, but the last 10% would take a lifetime (I'm paraphrasing). If we spend the first twenty years of our life figuring out the basics of eating, breathing, sleeping, physical and spiritual growth, social mores, education, career, ideologies and so on, then do we not spend the rest of our lives trying to perfect those things through practice and application?

In rowing *I* become the vessel; I empty myself, get out of my own way, so that I can be open to anything and everything free of limitation. Physically and spiritually I have a practice, a meditation that centers me. Hard work, repetition, mindfulness, pain, competition, sorrow, conflict, triumph, resolve, satisfaction, anger, passion, frenzy, dedication, depletion, violence, control, longing, exhaustion, and on and on and on – rowing is everything that makes life worth living, an epic odyssey lurking just beneath the surface of something so simple as moving a boat over water.

It occurs to me right now that if rowing has given me one thing in life it is focus. It has taught me the benefit of focus in conjunction with discipline and drive. Rowing has proved time and time again that I can do *anything* if I throw enough focus, discipline, and drive at it. My intent is to realize my potential as an athlete, even as a human being. The vehicle for that adventure is to train for the Olympic Trials. What I realize is that we have the potential to be practically limitless in our chosen capacities; an empty vessel. When we glimpse perfection, enlightenment, then we are no vessel at all. Maybe age is just such a vessel to be emptied.

"Once one is beyond a certain level of commitment to the sport, life begins to seem an allegory of rowing rather than rowing an allegory of life."

— Stephen Kiesling — *The Shell Game*

3/9/08: Rowing 5 seat in the San Diego 8+, I have no shortage of frustrations in my rowing, most notably skying my blade on the recovery and washing out through the drive. Scott will check the pitch on the rigger to see if something got tweaked.

Today we leave for Sacramento to train with the Sacramento State varsity in pairs at Lake Natoma. This is another benchmark. These benchmarks have been important reality checks for us. Our mutual understanding has been that if we should fail to meet a given benchmark we would hang the whole thing up and go home. After all, following one's dreams is a noble aspiration; being delusional is not. I had been emailing Brandon Hayes, the head coach at Cal State Sacramento. He will allow us to come down and train in pairs with his varsity men. Their racing season is already underway, so they are in peak condition. As I write this I remember the intensity of my collegiate varsity 4+ as we peaked for big races. The smoldering intensity of the four oarsmen of the apocalypse! Train, eat, train, eat, crush and kill, back to your cage.

I remember our stroke man, Kaj Halvorsen, announcing to the team after a particularly cold and grueling evening practice that he had broken up with his girlfriend as a gesture of his commitment to the crew and the Spartan training ethic. Steve wrote in The Shell Game,

"Outsiders think that rowing produces fanatics, but I think that potential fanaticism is just more recognizable when given a focus like rowing."

With our stealthy silver Hudson pair strapped to the top of my truck, Carl, Steve and I head south on a beautiful Sunday afternoon. Like many benchmarks before it, this would be the end of the story or the beginning of a new chapter. As I drive I think that I have no idea which way it will go. And I am okay with that.

11. BENCHMARK #4 – SACRAMENTO

3/10/08: 4:45 a.m. pulse — 48 beats per minute. At 5:30 a.m. we rig the pair at the CSUS boat house. By 6:00 a.m. lights are on, music is blasting, athletes are on ergs, doing calisthenics, clowning around, etc. The varsity gathers around Brandon as he assigns pair lineups. We will be in lane 1. His fastest pair will be in lane 2. This is a lightweight pair with sub 6:20 erg scores. I instantly recall watching a U.S. National Team video of heavyweight and lightweight pairs training together, and remember Steve's ominous words of caution, "Never race lightweights." Lanes 3, 4, and 5 make up the rest of his varsity 8.

The CSUS facility at Lake Natoma is one of the nicest in the country, easily one of the finest on the West Coast. We launch in complete darkness, heading down the outside of the 2,000-meter course and displacing all form of waterfowl. We are to race four 500-meter sprints, all with racing starts. Brandon calls the first in the darkness, quietly, "All hands are down. We have alignment. Attention ... Row!"

When I say we leapt off the line I mean we took a boat length in three strokes and another boat length in five. We had enough open water that it didn't matter when our steering cable dragged underwater and cranked the rudder over, steering us off course. We had fired the first shot across the port bow of the opposition. Hell, we *were* the shot across their port bow. Now we would await their reply.

Brandon addresses his athletes calmly but firmly, "You need to race these guys. I want you to take chances. Fix it or break it." The lightweight pair pushes us. By the third piece we are rowing a 1:36 split at 38 strokes per minute and it feels oddly comfortable and controlled. On the fourth piece we concede a 1 ½ boat length lead per Carl's suggestion. Remind me not to invite Carl to these things anymore. Brandon agrees that it will force us to keep the pressure on to the end. Down a boat length and a half, we go off the line at 43 strokes per minute, barely settling to 39 strokes per minute. Fifteen strokes from the finish we are bowball to bowball with the lightweights. And then it is over. Five boats. Four pieces. Four wins. Again, the adventure will continue.

The rest of the trip is just as successful, with excellent training pieces on the course that afternoon. Tuesday morning after a 2k warm-up, we do a 1000-meter sprint. This one gets the better of Steve, who confesses that he was just not mentally prepared to commit to that distance. I suggest a rolling start for the next piece to help us stay loose. We run our last 750 meters of the trip sub 1:45 at 34 to 35 strokes per minute and finish happy.

Maestro, a little perspective, please.

So, from an Olympic perspective, was that such a big deal? No, not really. It was just a step in a process; a marker along a path. And even at that, our markers are set within reach of where we want our path to take us, which is the trials, just short of the Olympics. But if we shift our perspective slightly, things change dramatically. Steve once said that, "If you told me when I was twenty years old that I would be competing with guys in their forties, I would have said you were nuts." But that is exactly what we just did. If we stop right this second and do nothing more, we have already affected a change in perception, in perspective, in reality. Wow! That is powerful. And here we thought we were just rowing a boat.

In this Peter Pan moment, Natoma is my Neverland and I can fly. In this moment, there is no "for a 41-year-old," or "for a 49-year-old". There are only athletes training with other athletes, pushing each other to achieve something greater than what their perceptions might currently allow, pushing each other to explore the boundary of what is, and pushing each other to dive deeper into the you of you for answers.

Lise points this out on Steve's blog; that what we are really doing is competing with our former selves. That quest may be more relevant than trying to compete against present day Olympians. When I was in college I competed against Sacramento State University. So to show up at Lake Natoma, 41 years old, and win four pieces in a row against the varsity tells me that yes, I can compete with my former self. And so can you. In fact, if you were not an athlete in your youth, the chances are even better that you can compete with your former self, even surpass your former self! The more deconditioned you are the greater your improvement will be. Maybe you have had a sedentary lifestyle for thirty years and now, in retirement, you can proclaim that you are in the best shape of your life. Maybe you were always in good shape and now, at 60, you are in as good a condition as you have ever been. How cool is that?

Case in point - My friend Cindy Bernard started rowing for the club in 2003. At 5'10" she is a perfect fit, seemingly destined to feature prominently on the WRT (women's racing team). But that was not happening. Her erg scores were not improving, she was fatigued and, whether 5'10" or 4'10", she was weak. Blood work showed severe anemia (genetic) and iron deficiency. She had asthma and needed an inhaler whenever she worked out. We got to work on a specific, low intensity, high volume aerobic program coupled with a high intensity, low volume strength program. When she started she could barely press five pounds. Now, five years later at 48 years old she is in the best shape of her life. She and pair/double partner Corrine Lombardi are a force to be reckoned with on the water. She now only uses the inhaler before 1,000 meter sprint races.

My agent, Stephany Evans, started running at 46 years old. Now 51, she has qualified for the Boston Marathon with a time of 4:04.34. I ask her if she is in the best shape of her life. She responds flatly, because it is email and because she is sick of me bugging her, "Yes, I'm in the best shape of my life. No question."

3/17/08: Buck the "isms". I've been thinking about all of these isms — sure, the obvious ones; racism, sexism, on-a-Saturday-I-can-live-on-chocolate-chip-cookies-and-milk-ism, and of course ageism. As I see it, everything is affected by relativism. That is the main ism. So you might say that we kicked some serious ism in Sacramento. But while I was gone, other heroes were kickin' Olympic caliber isms of their own.

Cap Capovilla was diagnosed with Parkinsonism in late October of 2007. His neurologist recommended an exercise program and Cap came to our gym (his wife Ruby was already there). This morning, after only five months, I came in to find a note on my desk informing me that Cap had been taken *off* his Parkinson's medication because of the positive effects of his exercise program.

Marceil Taylor, who comes in three times per week with great consistency and who Steve would call a "total babe," turned 93 in February. Marilyn Walker, our intrepid and unflappable human metronome on the erg, has lost 70 pounds over the last fourteen months. I got an email from Alfred Czerner, Olympian, world champion, CRASH B hammer and all around tuff guy, informing the club that he would not be at the San Diego Crew Classic this year. Alfred is in his early 70's, or early 170's, or somewhere in between. There is no actual proof or documentation as to his true age, only hearsay and folklore. So why, then, did old Alfred have to bail on the Classic — bad hip, ticker malfunction, revoked driver's license? Alfred had been invited to race in the Cotivel, an international single-scull sprint event in Lima, Peru! My heroes, one and all. Buck the isms!

"It's a great art is rowing. It's the finest art there is.
It's a symphony of motion.
And when you're rowing well, why it's near perfection.
And when you reach perfection, you're touching the divine.
It touches the you of you, which is your soul."

– George Pocock

3/24/08: Had a great talk with Andy Medcalf today. Given the speed of the lightweight pair at Sacramento, he sounded excited, if not a bit surprised, at our success down there. He asked how we were feeling. I said that Steve and I both felt that we peaked a bit for Sacramento, and were kind of fried. This week will be an aerobic recovery week, eleven hours of training at low intensity with only four to five 20-stroke starts on Wednesday for anaerobic work. Then we make our final charge of all-out, brutal, high-intensity workouts, leading us to peak on April 11. From there we will have a two-week taper to trials.

Medcalf says there will be between 12 and 15 national team

pairs at the trials, and that their strategy is to "push" at the 1000-meter mark. "So it's all about the third 500, then." He talks about "Speed without Fear." He likens it to a boxer. The boxer trains on the heavy bag, the speed bag, jumps rope, spars, looks at film, reads about the sweet science and so on. "But all that won't amount to a hill of beans once you step in the ring and some guy starts punching you in the face. It's just like rowing; thirty strokes in and theory goes out the window, it's a fight."

Steve calls this the "oh, shit" moment. This moment usually occurs about 30 strokes into a race, when your brain realizes that you have committed your body to do something that is terribly, horribly wrong. To know speed without fear you must immerse yourself in that terrible place and get comfortable with it. From an outsider's perspective, the fight is between the boats racing down the course to see who crosses the finish line first. What is truly, painfully obvious to all who dare to go there is that the real fight is within.

3/26/08: Monday we did a 40-minute and a 60-minute piece. Monday evening I was driving fence posts on my property. I love working outdoors, especially if I get to lift really heavy things or hit stuff. A fence post driver is a 28-pound steel cylinder with handles on it. I call it the Smasher. It is simple, ugly, purpose-built and effective; a big hammer. Maybe I should call it the Steve (I'll probably pay for that tomorrow).

Long story short, while driving the Smasher down I caught the top edge of the post and the Smasher came straight down on to my head with sufficient force as to rattle my teeth. I stood very still for a moment, knowing in the pit of my stomach that this was going to be bad. As my ears rang and the blood came down into my eyes I could see my wife running toward me with a towel.

Tuesday morning, 36 minutes into a 40 minute piece, I am experiencing nausea and double vision. A trip to the ER (pulse 50, bp 124/84) and a CT scan suggest that I have a concussion; the doctor recommends bed rest. *Bed rest!* Two weeks before we are to peak and every session counts and there is no time for this nonsense. And what kind of cosmic karmic crap is this and how exactly does *this* fit in the row-life parallel? I call Steve and tell him what happened. He laughs and identifies the truth of the situation, "that was stupid." We laugh together and I am comforted be his reaction. Precisely!

3/28/08: Wednesday we are supposed to do racing starts on the water. My new goal for Wednesday is to walk upright without vomiting. Thursday goes by without incident as I resign myself to the notion that I won't be working out. Now Friday morning, we take the pair out to do the race starts that should have been done on Wednesday. Rollers, wind and white caps.

We row at half slide, taking on water. Nothing of value will come of this. We try starts at half pressure, half speed. I am nauseous and my head hurts. Pointless, we take it back in at half slide so as not to flip, which we almost do anyway. At the boathouse, it is pretty clear that I am not ready to row yet. Pancakes and coffee sound much better. Says Steve, "In the grand scheme of things, forced rest is not such a bad idea."

On the phone Tammy says, "How many times have you told me that forced rest can be the best thing for you?" My sis-in-law says, "Don't mess with this; bed rest!" Andy Medcalf emails, "Remember, rest is good." So maybe that is the lesson, the epiphanic row-life parallel. Maybe sometimes you need to be hit over the head with it — Rest Is Good.

3/30/08: This morning we row the 8+ before de-rigging for San Diego; 22 degrees and snowing sideways. I couldn't feel my toes for an hour afterward, but what a great row!

3/31/08: I ask Steve if he is scared. He says he is both scared and cautiously optimistic. Today and tomorrow we will do 80 minutes of low-intensity erg work. Wednesday we will attack it on the water. On Wednesday the truth will be on the water. Not the entire truth, mind you, but a glimpse. Tammy, who I will now refer to affectionately as a Punk Buddhist Rebel, sent me this New Guinea Proverb: *Knowledge is just a rumor until it is in the muscle.*

Rowing is empowering on many levels. When Tammy went in for her first cancer surgery she did not have any symptoms. When she woke up from surgery she had many. That hardly seems fair. Strapped to her hospital bed, tubes and wires firmly affixed, her fear response was to rip free and run away, much like the "oh, shit" moment 30 strokes into a race. I am not trivializing cancer, only recounting Tammy's words, suggesting that empowerment isn't about victory but having the will, the strength to stay the course under traumatic conditions. When your hardwiring is telling you to bolt, your training overrides reason. Tammy says that rowing had prepared her, physically, mentally, spiritually, for cancer – truly empowering.

12. BENCHMARK #5 – SAN DIEGO

A reporter from the Associated Press (Dan Gelston) has picked up our story. He will write something in the coming days, and then come to the trials and cover them as well. Oh joy. I think this nervously, as there is no getting around the fact that the AP is huge.

I read a story written by Aquil Abdullah where he deftly recounts losing the 2000 single-scull Olympic trials by the smallest of margins (.33 second). I don't remember who beat him or how that person ended up doing at the Olympics. I just remember Abdullah's story. Steve reminds me of that, that what ended up being important to me was Abdullah's story, not the guy who went on. I don't pretend to be a threat to someone like Dan Beery who, by the way, is a really nice guy and blocks out the friggin' sun. But I do plan to be a guy who shows up to tell the story.

4/1/08: On the second 40-minute piece of the day Steve says, "I can't believe we're doing this." We both laugh nervously and I say "it's a little too late for that statement. You see, the cutoff date for that kind of statement is…um…THE DAY BEFORE THE A.P. GUY GETS THE STORY."

4/2/08: Wednesday, judgment day, 1000-meter pieces, make or break, do or die. More wind, more rollers, more bad water.

Not a very good workout. Nope. Forty strokes into the second 1k, Steve stops. Today he hangs from the dragon's tail, from the caboose. Steve is not having a pleasant time at this moment. George Sheehan once said that winning is, "never having to say 'I quit'". Right now my morale is saying that winning is never having to change my name and skip town, and I am not feeling like a winner. Tomorrow morning we are off to San Diego for the Crew Classic. This should be a good primer, timing-wise, for the trials. Now it seems the AP will have a photographer in San Diego. Steve tells them that we will be in an 8+, which is very different than the pair. Apparently that does not matter. Apparently our man from the AP knows nothing about rowing, by his own admission. He covers basketball out of Philadelphia. I think maybe they just need photographic proof that we are, indeed, old.

Fritz had suffered a setback; multiple back surgeries in the beginning months of 2008. He says that he is not currently "running" but "just jogging at a ten minute mile pace and riding my bike...really fast." It happened that in 2003 he received a gift. His colleagues from the 1977 Olympic Training Center at Squaw Valley had all gone on, as he had, to impressive careers. To show their appreciation, these men whom Fritz had mentored bought him a Trek racing bike, just like Lance Armstrong's. recounting this story to me over the phone, Hagerman says, "You know Lance wrote that book, *It's not about the bike*? Well trust me, at my age it's all about the bike!"

4/4/08: Steve, our stroke man Eric Glatte and I fly to San Diego this morning then head to Crown Pointe for lunch. This is ground zero for Spring Breakers. As such, nothing is open before 2:00 p.m. because it is mandatory that everyone still be in bed with hangovers.

As we get closer to the boardwalk there are some signs of life, and we get a sandwich at a place that probably doesn't do much business during the light of day. That afternoon we meet the rest of the guys and go out for a row to shake out the cobwebs. Steve is also rowing his rolodex 8+ chock full of Olympians, World Champions, National Teamers, and so on. It turns out their two seat, Tom Hull, is stuck on the tarmac in Houston, Texas and would I mind rowing port for a turnout?

Among the many really neat guys in this boat is Eric Stevens at 3 seat. Some of the very best rows I have ever had have been with Eric, so I jump at the chance. Eric is the stuff of legend and, more importantly, a really nice guy. I haven't rowed port for five years, so I just try to row clean and stay out of the way. Currently at 6'4" and 198 pounds, I am the second smallest guy in this boat, so 2 seat seems just right. As Steve would point out later, rolodex boats like this are only fun if you win. Otherwise it seems like an undue amount of tension and pressure - not the positive kind. You can feel it running throughout the boat. I have experienced this in other rolodex boats. Tension and pressure. Think about it. Unless you have a common bond, a history, a story, there is only the win. Take away the win, and what's left? Of course, if you row the same rolodex lineup again and again, it creates its own history. Anyway, I'm just filling in for a practice and I get to sit behind Eric, who is sitting behind Steve. When things get tense Eric cracks a joke quietly and we snicker like school kids. The impact of Eric's humility and self deprecation on the universe increases exponentially relative to his accomplishments and abilities. As Steve once said, "Eric, at his very worst, is barely mortal."

One of the unique rolodex boat dynamics is that you are dealing with individuals who have succeeded at the highest echelons of their sport. These are the men and women who have been where 99% of competitive athletes only dream of going. Each of them has followed a path with a goal at the end of it and reached that goal.

These are assertive, determined, strong willed individuals. When you put nine chiefs in a canoe without an Indian in sight, things can get a little tippy. When you win it's all great, because that was the goal of all parties involved; but if you don't win?

Then there is our Ashland Rowing Club 8+. Man did we have a great time! Rowing against San Diego, Potomac, Lake Union, Long Beach, Willamette and Marin, we performed within our race plan to finish third and qualify for the final, the fourth fastest time of both heats. That evening most of the team piled into Scott's crew cab to drive over to where the Women's team was cooking a huge dinner. On that drive, we all basically reverted to 13-year-olds' vomit humor, and I laughed so hard I cried. Too bad I didn't have milk. It would have shot out of my nose. I guess we were a bit giddy. There is something refreshingly cathartic about laughing yourself silly, no matter what the vehicle. I will never be able to think about this trip without it putting a big fat smile on my face. Thanks, guys.

Sunday's race plan was to be more aggressive. Starting in lane 6 based on a coin toss, we go out hard with 20 strokes high, settling 2 to 3 beats higher than we did in the heat. We know we have more than what we showed the day before. At the 1000 meter mark we push and it feels strong. We do not let up and Rocky Mountain can't stand the pressure. We are taking seats and they are unable to answer. Lake Union is open water behind. We are catching Pocock, who won last year. At 1600 meters we take our sprint, still powerful, a bit ragged, but still very aggressive. With 200 meters to go we have overtaken Pocock. Convergent water, wind, and plain old bad lane 6 juju pushes us into the lane markers. Somewhere in that finite piece of real estate Rich, our 2 seat and orator of vomit stories smacks a buoy with his oar blade. It is just enough of a momentum shift. Pocock crosses the line 3/10 of a second ahead of us for third place. Marin takes second to

Long Beach who wins in spite of, or possibly because of, one of their oarsmen dying in the boat two weeks prior.

We end up in fourth place — by 3/10 of a second. Dam... well...that was... so much $#%^&#* *fun!* It was a battle and we were *in it*! We did not back down. We attacked from start to finish. It was ugly but effective enough and we had a wicked third 500 and sometimes you just have to jump right in there and get scrappy and sometimes that's just the way it is and I'd do it again tomorrow and I know you would too so who's got frequent flyer miles? I've got some Cytomax residue left in my water bottle but not *that* water bottle cause I peed in it and come to think of it so did you. *Who's with me? Go Ashland!*

4/8/08: On the plane ride home we share the flight with the Saint Ignatius High School crew team from San Francisco. My dad went to Saint Ignatius. Actually he was kicked out of Saint Ignatius. His junior year he wrote a paper listing ten reasons why religion was fallible. He told them he was going to write it. They told him not to. He wrote it and was expelled. Seventeen years old with no high school diploma, too young to enlist in the Army in the midst of a world war, he was in a tight spot. Stanford, it seemed, was also in a tight spot. They needed students in a bad way. Theirs were off fighting a world war. Surely this noble establishment of learning and this assertive, determined, strong willed individual could reach an agreement?

At 17 years of age, young Alfred Baxter started his freshman year at Stanford University, with philosophical dragons to slay and mountainous worlds to conquer and rose lipped maidens to woo. He worked in the kitchen, I imagine with the same integrity and gumption that he applied to every other facet of his life. This was the superhero way.

13. LETTING GO

4/10/08:   Yesterday we are on the water for two times 1000-meter pieces.   Steve and I argue about the stroke coach. Steve's argument is that by paying attention to our splits we limit ourselves to what we think we are capable of.   I argue that the stroke coach is there to prevent us from going out too hard, getting too deep in the pain tank, and dying.   After our warm-up, I am uneasy.   I have a sense of dread that this is going to get ugly.   We sit ready for our first piece, 5-15-115.   That is a 5-stroke race start, 15 high, then 115 strokes. We go out fast. Very fast. Too fast.   Twenty strokes in and the dread is enveloping me.   There is a fogginess in my brain and the fight or flight queasiness that comes from being backed into a corner, deciding whether to throw the first punch or bolt for the exit and knowing that neither choice is on my terms.   I catch a glimpse of the stroke coach –1:32. 1:32! That's insane. I'm not going to make it. I think, "I can't keep this up. I can't do this." Damn it! I cave in to the pain and the fear. Collapsing inward, I stop. I am so tight that I can't sit up, can't breathe.

Steve is as happy as a kid in a sand box. He thinks it feels light and quick and effortless. He is just tooling along and can't figure out why I have stopped. He doesn't look at the stroke coach. He isn't influenced by external indicators. He is just going by feel. "Well, that's enough of that." He reaches forward and shuts off the stroke coach monitor. He may as well have thrown it in the lake. The time for external indicators is over.

While talking about the trials with the rolodex coxswain in San Diego he said, "No more thought. Just do. Now you are the machine."

We line up again. Light and quick. Light and quick. *Feel* the boat. 5-15-115. Sixty strokes in and I can't hear anything. Whoosh, chunk. Whoosh, chunk. Are we even touching the water? Don't think. Just do. I am the machine. One hundred thirty-five strokes later there is no heaving, no cramping, only the palpable sense that something very special is going on here. The second piece is the same. Don't make the boat go faster by pulling harder. That is what you *think* you should be doing. Just pulling hard makes you tight, short and tired, just like nationals in Seattle. Let go. Let go of what you *think* you should be doing. Let go of the numbers, the splits, the stroke rate, the theory, the baggage. We are no longer rowing a boat, two bodies, two oars in a shell on a body of water. We are the boat. We are the water. We are omnipresent and invisible, a powerful force and terribly fragile. Quite possibly, briefly, we are enlightened. We *are* the machine. Two weeks to trials and I am still deconstructing, exhausted, vulnerable, and getting closer to the truth.

As we recover from the second piece, a bald eagle lands in a barren tree. An osprey is trying to force the eagle away. The eagle pays no attention, doesn't even flinch. The osprey leaves as quickly as it shows up. The eagle stares.

I say, "Look at the eagle."

Steve, breathless, "That's not an eagle, that's a spirit eagle."

"A what?"

"A spirit eagle. What we've just done is a major event; a transition. The spirit eagle is here as a sign of recognition."

"Really?"

"Yeah, well you can make the story whatever you want, but at this point I'll take whatever I can get."

Amen to that. If you systematically beat the crap out of yourself for a year and a half, you are bound to find religion somewhere.

"You've got to lay it all out there, stagger home, sit down to dinner with your wife and say 'honey, I've got to push harder tomorrow."

– Andy Medcalf

4/13/08: 2000 meters blind. No stroke coach. This morning we rehearse everything from the dock to the last stroke of an all out 2k. Medcalf says that we won't get more than 30 minutes warm-up at the trials, so we better have this whole thing mapped out. Nothing too dramatic here. We had a clean start and the boat felt light and quick. The third 500 meters, sometimes referred to as "the graveyard", felt surprisingly good. The final 500 lacked punch, which will be addressed. We took a clean up 10 at the 500-meter mark and a power 20 at the 1000-meter mark, but made no plans for the last 500 meters. We cross the line, ironically, at the cemetery, in 7:24. We will put in a power 30 at the 1750 mark for our sprint. What matters most is that it didn't fall apart. We definitely owned it, and that was a great confidence builder.

4/15/08: The sucking sounds of the taper. Tapering sucks. You are used to expending a certain amount of energy per day, and to take that away while at the same time mentally on *high alert* as your train is reaching terminal velocity is just plain evil. We were going to race another 2k this Sunday, but Medcalf advised against it. Rather, we will do two 1k's with 20 minutes' rest in between. Tomorrow (Wednesday) we will do three times 500's, then Thursday we will do four times 300's, then light on Friday.

The time trial is done on a rolling start, meaning we will go across the starting line at speed. Once in Princeton we will have two and a half days to get our boat and oars dialed in. Thursday night there will be an athlete meeting; Friday morning is the time trial. In discussing strategy, Medcalf recommends putting our best effort into the time trial. If we place too low we will be forced to race twice the first day. If we can place in the top eighteen we will get to rest until Saturday morning. Of course, if we have our best row ever in the time trial and finish dead last because we are old, weak and slow then we will race twice the first day anyway and be getting older and weaker and slower with every passing stroke. And that, also, would be what it is.

Okay, so I broke down and hammered out four times 2000 meters on the erg. Just laid into 'em. Way too much energy on deck. I'm probably going to pay for that. That is a classic Steve move, when in doubt kick the crap out of yourself on the erg. What day is it? Tuesday. We leave in exactly one week. I may want to give up coffee for a while. I may want to perform some deep breathing exercises. I may want to mainline horse tranquilizers and bash myself over the head with a fence post driver. I am starting to smolder. The apocalypse is near.

Leah Wingfield, club member, world-renowned artist, hammer and happy camper sent out this email:

Our resident Olympic hopefuls, Andy Baxter and Steve Kiesling, are off to Princeton next week to compete in the Olympic trials!

Join them, THURSDAY, APRIL 17 - STANDING STONE - 5:00 pm. for a club send-off.

Buy them a beer, but not too many, they're in training :-P Give them a pat on the back, but not too hard, you don't want to injure them. ;-)

Refrain from making jokes about their age, you don't want to upset them˘ —: —

* Come, raise a glass, and wish them flat water and strong leg drives! 8-)

4/16/08: Pain and suffering revisited. Today's 500's hurt. These are not like the 500's in Sacramento. These are mad. There are no grand epiphanies. No eagles fly out to check on our progress. There is only pain. This is what Medcalf had in mind when he spoke of pain and suffering. There are no relevant measurements. The point is to attack it with such ferocity that it is completely unrealistic. The intent is to willfully put yourself in harms way. The goal is to immerse yourself in that dark and terrible place and see what looks back at you. As the John Gable poster says, "Great challenges offer the greatest rewards. How we meet them reveals the truth in all of us." The truth hurts. We spill out of the boat, collapsing onto the dock. Carrying the boat back to the boathouse I fight the urge to vomit. I am too tired to vomit. I might drop the boat. Otherwise I would welcome it.

"There is advantage in the wisdom won from pain."

— Aeschylus

.

4/17/08: I don't remember going to bed last night. This morning we are back at it, four times 300 meters. This workout allows us to focus on specific elements of our race plan — the start and settle (lengthen), the body with a power 20 at the 1000-meter mark, and the sprint at the finish. These pieces are everything they should be; crisp, light, strong, economical and fast. Steve says, "That might be the best we have ever rowed." I agree. We have been rowing and racing the pair together for five years. Then, six days before we leave for the Olympic trials, we find another level. Fourteen months of training for these precious few moments.

64 weeks. 576 hours. 34,560 minutes, approximately 700,000 strokes. 2,857 strokes taken for each stroke in the race. 4,937 training minutes for each minute in the race. This morning, with no one to see it, we flew. And that makes it worth every one of the 2,073,600 seconds.

At Fifty years old, Mom went back to school, earning a Masters Degree in architecture from Cal Berkeley. She celebrated by doing an "all girl" outward bound trip. The photo on my brother's fridge stands as proof that fifty year old mountaineer legs are every bit as sinewy and muscular as twenty year old mountaineer legs. In our house you would never question why one might throw a few volumes of the Oxford English Dictionary into a back pack and head up to Grizzly Peak for a hike. She also took up running and was absolutely hooked. Her own personal meditation space was at the Deaf and Blind school track, above the Cal dorms. That was her spiritual pilgrimage. She made it religiously. When throat cancer came calling, she kept running. She never thought to stop, and that is why she is my hero.

4/19/08: Thursday night we went to our club send off party; drank beer, ate pizza and fought off the urge to crawl under the table and sleep. The club had a donation box to help pay for our expenses. If we fail will they want their money back? I guess the only way to fail would be to not show up. This morning, in freezing weather and a headwind, we raced two times 1000 meters, staggered start against all sorts of club boats – doubles, quads, a four, etc. In hindsight, I think the party was a ploy to fill us with pizza and beer so that all others would have an advantage this morning. Great fun had by all. What a wonderful group of people. Coach Joe presented us with ARC shirts that say Old Guys Rule on the front. If I didn't row I'd be naked. I would be stripped of my identity, physically and spiritually, lost in a sea of ambiguity and suffocating beneath the weight of my own purposeless existence. I also get my shirts at regattas.

Steve had started the Ashland High School girls program in the fall of 1998. By Spring of 2000 the grownups wanted a piece of the action. There was a town hall meeting. About 40 people showed up, Jim Sims and Marty Thommes among them. Steve would pass the president hat to Marty and the head coaching hat to Jim. RowAshland was formed, thus master's rowing in the Southern Oregon valley. RowAshland would later become Ashland Rowing Club. Every year at our annual Ashland Rowing Club banquet, three awards are given. These are the Kiesling Cup, celebrating the Joy of Rowing; the Jim Sims award, celebrating the Competition of Rowing, and the Tao of Thommes, celebrating the Team Spirit and Unity of Rowing. Joe Lusa would come later as assistant coach, and then take on head coaching duties.

There is an enormous supporting cast of characters in the Ashland Rowing Club, whose membership runs about 120 currently. Considering the town population of 21,630, Steve proposes that

Ashland has the most successful rowing club, per capita, in the United States. If you are ever in town, give us a call and decide for yourself (www.ashlandrowingclub.org).

14. STEVE, ANDY AND THE GIANT BUZZ SAW

Originally the idea of going to the trials was part of a grand and romantic notion that during an Olympic year *anyone* can take their best shot. During a non-Olympic year it does not work that way. You have to make and be a part of the national team first to compete at the highest level. Our thought was that the 8+ and the 4- would already be selected. The biggest of the big dogs would already have their seats, and could look down from the pantheon as lesser mortals showed up with heady Olympic dreams, or even just to see how they stacked up. NYAC, Penn AC, Vesper, California Training Center, University of Washington, Cal, Wisconsin, Harvard, and Yale and so on — surely they would have athletes coming. *That is what this is all about, right?*

Well, two things do not go according to our grand and romantic notion. The first is that the Big Boats have not been officially selected. The national team gods will use the pair trial as a tool for big boat selection. Fourteen national team pairs will be on hand. The fastest six pairs will be selected for big boat camp. Twenty-eight elite physiological freaks (Fritz's words) will plunge, headlong, as deep as they have ever gone into the pain tank to win one of 12 seats in the 8+ and the 4- to represent our country in the Olympic Games. That is no joke. That is fighting for your life. That is not our fight.

And what is the second thing that did not quite go according to our plan? What is the chink in my philosophical row-life parallel armor? *Nobody showed up*! Seventeen boats registered. Not even enough to mandate a time trial. Fourteen national team pairs, a well credentialed Michigan pair, a pair from Vesper ... and us. I phone Steve with the news, to which he responds, "I think we just trained for a year and a half to walk right in to a giant buzz saw."

4/21/08: I spend Sunday in a complete haze, basically worthless in thought and action. I can't focus on anything, trying to wrap my head around all of this. One year ago I wrote that so much of the row-life parallel was showing up. Tomorrow morning we will get on an airplane and put that philosophy to the test.

Now it looks like Vesper has added another pair. That makes eighteen boats. If there was one more boat, that would be ugly. The slowest boat would be the odd man out. With nineteen boats, one pair would have a very short weekend. With nineteen boats, *we* would probably have a very short weekend. Hmm.

So as I struggle through my day with my thoughts in tow, I receive an email. It is from Jacque, my friend who just happens to have a day job as my manager and also serves as one of my most trusted confidants. The email subject line reads "a wise man once said..." I open the email. What I see on the screen moves me. It is a metaphysical sucker punch that I never could have seen coming.

"I'm not here to conquer the mountain. I'm here to conquer myself."

Alfred W. Baxter quoting Sir Edmund Hillary's "we are not here to conquer the mountain, but ourselves." Jacque had picked it up from some notes I had made for an industry trade show we went to in Florida.

Damn, she's good. Damn. Clearly I am not paying her enough. Damn.

15. ATTENTION

4/22/08: Nineteen boats. The U.S. has added another pair, bringing the total to nineteen. The time trial will be the race of our lives. Nothing really changes except that a defeat would be *glaring*.

4/23/08: From Jim Millar's house on Carnegie Lake, New Jersey, we pull the Hudson pair down and rig on the dock. Focusing on not dropping any nuts or washers (which I do — sorry, Jim) the first pair comes lumbering into view. The bowman is wearing a black singlet. On the back, in small white letters — USA. This is our coast of South Africa and these are the great whites. One by one they go by, the predatory fish of the U.S. National Team. One by one we say hi and good morning, recognizing most by face and a few by name. Surprisingly, they seem to recognize us as well; Probably the YouTubes. Cameron and Tyler Winklevoss row close enough to the dock to say, "Good luck guys, but not too much." They are identical twins and I could not tell you which one said it. With fifteen national team pairs among nineteen pairs competing for eighteen spots, I assure him that we are just here for comic relief. But we are here.

4/24/08: Finn Caspersen Olympic Training Center – there is a commotion in one of the boat bays. It is immediately apparent that the commotion is for us. A small film crew is setting up lights and equipment for a photo shoot. In 1982 Steve had his photo taken in Andy Warhol's *Interview* magazine. Among other things, these guys planned to recreate that photo, twenty-six years later. The embarrassing thing about this is that, while present-day Olympians and World Champions surround us, we are getting an inversely proportionate amount of attention relative to our abilities. It is oddly absurd, which is fitting. The whole thing is absurd. Sebastian Bea walks by and says casually, "You know our film crew will be here any minute, they're just running a little bit late."

I introduce myself to Bryan Volpenhein. He and Jason Read are the fastest pair on the team. Bryan, coincidently, is the oldest guy on the team. I give him a shirt from my gym, which says "Out of my way, Sonny" on the front. Looking around I say, "You know, all of this … we're just gonna do our thing and stay out of your way." He says, "No, I think what you are doing is great. Have a great race!"

Matt Madigan, Potomac and Olympic sculling coach, is here with his women's doubles. It turns out that Matt and I rowed against each other in the early nineties — he at Santa Clara, I at Humboldt. He says, "You guys have put in the time and the strokes. You have as much right to be here as everyone else." This is comforting, as at this moment I am feeling like a complete idiot. Carl asks Madigan if he is still rowing. "No way, between marriage and kids on one side and coaching and rowing on the other, I am only allowed one of the other!" Amen, brother. I feel your pain.

Athlete meeting with U.S. Olympic Committee and USRowing. USRowing states that if you or your representative is not present at role call, you will be disqualified. Michigan is a no show. They are officially scratched. Eighteen boats. We are in! We will now be able to use tomorrow's time trial as a race rehearsal. Tomorrow night at 6:40 p.m. we will line up, head to head, shoulder to shoulder, and stroke for stroke with the best athletes in the country, some of the best in the world. This is everything we ever wanted in our journey, and we got it because we showed up! And that, dear readers, is the row-life parallel. We later find out that Michigan did show up, but then the national team pair of Kyle Larson and Sam Burns had to scratch due to Sam pulling a muscle in his back.

Now, as originally planned, we will use the time trial as an introduction to the course. Figuring that we have only one really good race in us, we will conserve energy and use this piece to get the jitters out. There is a small circular warm up pattern to the side of the first 500 meters. Back here there is no access, by car or on foot. There are no spectators. In college I had a bumper sticker that read, "On the water, no one can hear you Scream...Humboldt Crew." For this occasion I might modify that message to, "Scream all you want. These are the Olympic Trials." The imagery of circling sharks is obvious. Are we circling with them or are they circling us?

The time trial will be two lanes with staggered starts. Bow markers, white plastic cards with numbers on them that fit to the front of the boat, designate the order in which we will start. As we get closer to the start time two things are gravely clear. The first is that esprit de corps is morphing into every pair for themselves. The frenzied sharks are starting to snap at each other and a pecking order is emerging. What had been jovial wisecracking is now "shut up, do your job and get out of my way." The second thing that is now ridiculously clear is that Steve and I are late and out of order. Now we are the new kid in school at the back of the bus hoping that the driver will stop at his stop so that he doesn't have to get up and pull the chord and draw attention to himself but of course the driver is not going to stop so he pulls the chord and every other kid turns around and glares and he stumbles down the crowded aisle whacking every other kid with his cumbersome backpack, "Sorry, 'scuse me, ouch, sorry…" Snapping sharks barely tolerate our breaking through the ranks.

Getting off the line, onto the course, and out of that melee is emancipating. It is a fantastic morning; there is no wind, and no pressure on us. In fact, we practically row at no pressure. We are cruising at 70% power, focusing on staying long and breathing well and keeping a straight course. It is the greatest feeling in the world. We get to row in perfect conditions at the Olympic training center with the best athletes in the world but without the gut wrenching, soul twisting pain of a real race. Their reality is quite different. With the pecking order always being challenged, the sharks will use the time trial to jockey for position in the heats.

Around the 1000-meter mark Ted Nash is on the shore propped against his bicycle, "Come on Steve, atta boy!" We smile and wave and say "Hi" as we cruise along. At this point a parasol and some Brie and crackers would be appropriate. In the lane next to us we had been watching a pair for some time. We are all racing the clock, so to speak (that row/life parallel doesn't really need to be pointed out, does it?), so their race is separate from ours. But as we near the final 500 meters, it is clear that the Winklevoss twins are cranking it up for the sprint. "Let's hold them off," I say. This is not fair at all, as they are going full tilt and we have been playing in the sun and couldn't be fresher, but how often would we get a chance to match strokes with the best? We build pressure and rate and ramming speeding and unload everything and it feels great and, even though it is a thoroughly uneven playing field, we hold them off through the finish line. Life is but a dream.

One reason for the restricted access to the beginning of the race course is that it is bordered by a private golf course. Steve, Carl, and I set out on a reconnaissance mission to somehow get Carl within camera view of the start. Exploration on foot proves futile, unless we are gauging success by tick accumulation, in which case this outing is a tremendous success. We abandon the idea of crawling around in the bushes thigh deep in water. Instead we will follow a radically different tack; we will act like grown-ups, go to the swanky golf club and ask permission to access the shoreline from their grounds. The swanky golf club guy goes above and beyond the call, providing us with two golf carts and a security escort. Once we have found the right spot, it is agreed that Carl will return in the evening and be given full access as well as a golf cart to get around in.

Back at the boathouse, lane assignments for the heats have been listed on the board. The three slowest boats, of which we are one, are split between the heats. We draw the fastest heat. That is perfect. Go big or go home, right?

Andy Medcalf takes us aside and says, "This is a once in a lifetime chance to do something that most guys will never get to do. You are going to go to the line with the best. Enjoy it."

16. ROW

4/25/08: This is it. We nap. We brood. We itch with the anticipation of, well, everything. No more thought, just do. The wind continues to pick up. The sharks circle around us. Is that rain? I am not numb. I am not scared or nervous. I just am. Energy, energy, energy ... let's do this thing.

Headwind; three-quarter headwind. Chop. We are in the fastest heat - Volpenhein and Read, Olympic Champions from the 8+ in 2004. Beery and Boyd, the fastest pair from NSR #1. The lead sharks, the dominant predators. Our number one priority — maintain contact as long as we can. The judge calls the lineup from lane 1 to lane 6, "U.S. Rowing Training Center, Volpenhein; U.S. Rowing Training Center, Inman; U.S. Rowing Training Center, Liwski; U.S. Rowing Training Center, O'Dunne; U.S. Rowing Training Center, Boyd; Ashland Rowing Club ..." deafening silence, holding breath, the light turns green, the horn sounds, we go. Five-stroke start then 20 high, then settle, but we don't settle and 20 becomes 30, then 40, then 50. This is battle. It is ragged and rushed and ugly and that is what it takes to stay on the stern deck of Micah Boyd and Dan Beery for 600 meters. That is what it takes. The headwind should give me the advantage over Steve, and in any other race it might have. Not today. Steve is, quite simply, attacking. He is attacking the water, our opponents, me, the setting sun. Steve is attacking his own mortality. I am fighting for my life and losing. I am hanging from the demons tail. Steve is the demon. I can't compete with the demon gear. He pulls me into lane 5. Shit. We have no rudder. I don't recall this being part of the race plan. We are riding the lane markers between 5 and 4 in a straight line but I can't pull us back. I do not cave in to the pain and the fear, quite the opposite. I am eating it up. I actually have the image of chewing on the pain. No pain. Know pain. No fear. Know fear. I am killing my demon when it matters most. This could be the greatest race of my life. Unfortunately, simultaneously, Steve's demon, Steve, is killing me. So I have to concede defeat to the one person in the universe who is supposed to be my ally. I focus every neuron, every molecule of oxygen on the effort to speak, "Come on, man, get me out of here." And right then and there I know that he is thinking, when it mattered most, he picked the wrong guy. When it mattered most, I have let him down.

Somewhere after 1000 meters Steve starts to tank. There is some sort of settle in the boat. Steve is starting to fall apart. I am regaining some clarity, some confidence. In the last 500 meters I speak again, this time to encourage him on. We finish the race in lane 5. Incredulously, I get the handshake. What the hell just happened? What the hell was that? I am as emotionally drained as I am physically. No, more emotionally drained. I trained for the physical part. The grand paradox of this event is that in fifteen years of pulling an oar, and after all of that drama, we finish dead last and I am still elated. Right at that moment I'm probably just elated because it is over and I survived, even if barely. With the headwind as bad as it was, there were not going to be any personal bests this evening. The water was perfect for the time trial, but we coasted through that. So this was it. We had before us the truly incredible opportunity to do something that few would ever get the chance to do. So we went like hell, lasted 600 meters, gassed out and hung on to cross the line, no rudder, big headwind, in 7:55. Volp and JR won in 6:54. We pulled a Tiff, although he had suggested 400 meters and we managed to hang on a bit longer. We hung around the finish line to thank every boat for a great race. All are gracious. Jason Read, bowman in the winning pair, says "It's an honor to go to the line with you guys." Amidst the manure that is a pony moment.

There will be an A, B and C final. Only the winner of the A final will move on to the Munich World Cup. We have the option of rowing in the C final in the morning or going downtown for beer, burgers, and chocolate brownie sundae deserts. We pass on the C final, which posts times from 7:27 to 8:02. I think we figured we had had enough, although after seeing those times compared to our 7:55 fly-and-die in a headwind, we should have showed up for that one too. That is easy for me to say now.

Sunday morning, Carl, Steve and I stand in the drizzle at the last 100 meters for the A final. Volpenhein and Read win by open water, with Boyd and "the Hurricane" Beery in second. Volp and JR will be the representative 2- to take a shot at the Olympic qualifier in Munich. As they paddle by the shore I bow in "we're not worthy" fashion. Volp looks up, points at me and says, "Out of my way, Sonny!" Ponies as far as the eye can see.

We drop Carl at Newark airport then head in to Manhattan. We have some time before our flight and the *New York Times* had run our story in the Sunday edition. What better time to go to New York to buy a newspaper and a cup of coffee? I call my friend Curt Schmidt while walking along Bleecker Street. Curt and I were friends, fellow musicians and personal trainers in New York while attending NYU a lifetime ago. I tell him that, although it might sound weird, I had just come from the Olympic trials and I am currently standing in the West

Village looking at myself in the sports section of the *New York Times*. Curt says, "That doesn't sound weird at all. Actually that sounds normal for you." I guess I haven't changed all that much over the years.

My dad passed away in March of 2005. Speaking in his honor at the UC Berkeley Faculty Club, I said that "all of our successes, and glorious failures, in life existed because our parents presented to us early on the ideal that anything was possible. We just had to go out and do it. In response to proposed adventures as varied as the disciplines and passions that we were encouraged to pursue, Dad would say, 'I hope this brings you great joy, and not your ultimate destruction.' Such was the sage advice of the superhero dad. He knew first-hand that the potential downside to the big climbs could be big falls, and he tried gently to warn us, as any good super hero dad would." I named our Hudson pair the Alfred W. Baxter and donated it to the club. We christened it at the boathouse. I am sure that he would have thought that to be a terrible waste of perfectly good champagne.

The day after our heat we go back to Princeton Training Center to row the pair back to Jim's house on Carnegie Lake. The Princeton frosh/novice 8 is celebrating a victory over Yale and Cornell in the Carnegie Cup. We rig anonymously at water's edge while teammates embrace for photos and parents witness their sons becoming young men right before their eyes. We slip away from the dock and head under the bridge into the wind with long, deliberate, relaxed strokes. The sights and sounds of the Princeton boathouse and youthful jubilation fade and soon we are alone again - the boat, the body, the water, the machine.

Jim had just been telling me how this lake can have a big wind that does not upset the water's surface much at all. I am grateful for the headwind, as I don't want this row to end. When it is over our journey is over. Our train will come to a gentle stop at its final destination, while the tracks that got us there, physically, spiritually, emotionally, were not always so gentle. Our rhythm, rock solid in the headwind, is trancelike. I am thinking of the F. Scott Fitzgerald line from The Great Gatsby and Steve says it, "So we beat on, boats against the current, borne back ceaselessly into the past."

So what did we accomplish? We trained hard and diligently, coming as close as either of us had ever come to our peak fitness as younger men. We had also found out what Fritz already knew — athletes continue to get stronger and faster. If the 1964 U.S. Olympic champions were transported to the present to race the 2004 U.S. Olympic champions, the '64 crew would get their clocks cleaned.

We created a story that people rallied around and, thanks to youtube.com and row2k.com, found out that its' appeal was universal. We raced and lost to the very best athletes our country had to offer. We showed up, didn't get laughed at too much, and possibly put the notion into someone else's head, "Hey, those guys did it. I'll bet we can do it too!" In fact that did happen. Susan Francia and Anna Goodale, who have earned their spots on the women's 8+ bound for Beijing, told us they were already talking about how cool it would be to come back to the trials in twenty years (they also told us that we looked good at 12 strokes per minute, another massive pony moment!). We were one of the first pebbles thrown in the pond, one of the first flaps of the butterfly's wings!

There is discussion as to what the next great adventure will be. Steve wants to get a new kayak and there is also talk of a world-class whitewater rafting competition. My brother and I now have a donor vehicle (thanks, Lise) that we want to prep for the Baja 500. My wife Denise, son Garrett and daughter Aubrey (now six years old) continue to grow into evermore-beautiful people in their own diverse ways, so I get to enjoy and share in that. Possibly I need to expand my level of consciousness by diving into oceans yet uncharted in my experience. Mankind hates and fears what he does not understand, and rarely do we understand what we hate and fear. Rather then perpetuate the bigotry and prejudice of ignorance and its hateful and fearful entanglements; I will take the enlightened moral high ground. I will embrace what heretofore I have known to be evil and wrong and fundamentally sinister in its foundations. I will try sculling.

17. STUNNED SURVIVORS

7/15/08: With all train wrecks there is an aftermath. Smoke must clear, perspective must be reestablished, damage assessed. Survivors stumble about, trying to comprehend dramatic and traumatic changes in speed, in energy, in emotion, in reality, in your understanding of life and death. Loved ones are cautiously optimistic, knowing that something about your cosmic bubble has changed in size or color or texture, but not yet knowing whether they are on the inside or the outside of that bubble. Denise has seen it before. We have talked through it before. It helps to know what to expect.

When we first got home I was honestly shocked to hear some people's responses. They would say, "I am so sorry that you didn't make it to the Olympics. You must be so heartbroken." They would console me and say, "Remember that it's the experience that counts." I knew from day one that I didn't have a legitimate shot at the Olympics and I knew from day one that it was the experience that counted, and if they knew that also, they would not be trying to console me. It was then that the shell-shock truly set in because I knew that others could not understand. I wouldn't truly be able to share this with anyone... except Steve.

As with most train wrecks, no two people see the event the same way. Steve and I may have experienced some ruffles as to the way that the A heat played out, but the train ride in this experience and the scenery that came with it carry far more importance and meaning than even its tumultuous anticlimax or its gentle stop at Jim Millar's dock in Princeton. I have to believe that. Things were said, opinions were argued, feelings were hurt. Time passed. Occasionally we would talk on the phone, sheepishly admitting to each other that we weren't training that much, or eating that well, or staying away from the spirits usually associated with victory.

Yesterday Steve called me. "You want to row a rolodex 4+ at Nationals with Mike Gasper and Stormy (Mark Stormberg)?" They are members of the rolodex Rocky Mountain 8+. Normally my Pavlovian response would be to shout, "Hell yes," then lie, cheat and steal my way into making it happen. With less than five weeks before the 2008 US Masters National championships in Long Beach, California, I sigh in resignation, "I'm gonna have to pass. I'm out of shape, and going would break my promise to Denise." I had told Denise that after the trials I would take a break from rowing for a full season. I had told her that before, many times. This was the first time that I had actually kept my word. I was biking a lot, having built up a new fixed gear track bike from SOMA Fabrications, and I was running with Denise occasionally. But that was not, nor could it be compared to, rowing. Steve says, "Yeh, I was kind of thinking the same thing." I look at my calendar. "I have an opening at 2:00 p.m., you want to come in and work out, just for fun?" I figure that this is just more lip service, as we had tried unsuccessfully to meet for workouts in the previous weeks. I get the feeling that this is more like the chatter of two estranged friends saying "we should really get together sometime and catch up…" never to see each other again.

At 2:00 p.m. sharp Steve walks in wearing trou and a t-shirt, his pants and shoes cradled in the supine palm of one hand (normally you would carry them under your arm, but when you are as big as

Steve, that would look cartoonish and stupid, much like wearing a fence post driver on your skull). We work out on the ergs and then exhaust ourselves under the weight of the Smith machine doing squats.

I write this at midnight, a burnt orange moon behind me. Garrett, no doubt dreaming musical dreams and Aubrey, with new rat Clyde, sleep peacefully. Denise knows I won't stop until I finish this. She too has gone to bed. Steve and I will train for the Head of the Charles in the fall, and I will cherish the warmth and reception of Dave and Johanna Potter's floor.

"Far better it is to dare mighty things, to win
Glorious triumphs, even though checkered by
Failure, than to take rank with those poor
Spirits who neither enjoy much nor suffer
Much because they live in the gray twilight
That knows neither victory nor defeat."

– Theodore Roosevelt

(Teddy probably would have rowed the pair - by himself.
Teddy was a badass.)

18. BACK TO BOSTON

10/20/08: I thought that I had the perfect ending; that by leaving you with the gang and me on Potter's floor you could come up with your own "ride off into the sunset" moment. But, as truth is so often way more fun than fiction, I had to come back and tell you what happened in Boston.

Like any other year at the Charles, lineups are juggled and nothing is certain. Dave Potter gets recruited to stroke the Bulldog 8+. Steve is obligated to attend a conference for his magazine, *Spirituality & Health*, and will not be able to go to Boston at all. Scott's dad's health is in decline and he must see to that. I guess that it just wasn't meant to be this year. There is a reason for everything. This is probably the universe's way of telling me that it is time to grow up, to focus my attention on more stable pursuits. After all, we are in the midst of the second worst economic downturn in our Nation's history. The last thing I need is to go traipsing off to the other end of the country to mess about in boats. I feel better already. Haaaa. Hmmm. Yep. This is nice.

Steve calls. The Rocky Mountain boys are putting together a rolodex 4+. Am I interested? "Hell yes!" I stuff some clothes in my backpack, small backpack; not many clothes. If I fly through the night on Thursday from Medford to San Francisco to Philadelphia to Boston I could be there by morning. Then I could take the Silver line to the subway and the subway to Harvard Square. From Harvard Square I could walk down JFK Drive to the Charles River, over Anderson Bridge, then upriver to Northeastern's Henderson boathouse. There I could meet Mike Gasper, Mark Stormberg, Harry Graves and coxswain Raedene Keeton. We could have our first and only practice together in a shiny new Empacher racing shell provided by Larry Gluckman of Trinity University. Then I could run back downriver to the Harvard boathouse to meet Fritz, who would be testing the '72 guys. I could test with Fritz, then make my way downtown in time to grab a bite to eat then sleep on the hotel room floor in Mike and Stormy's room. We could get up in the morning and race, then I could hightail it back to the airport, catch multiple flights, and be home in time to tuck the kids in. Oh, this is totally doable!

So that's what I did. We rigged the Empacher around 3:00 pm outside the Northeastern boathouse. Introductions were made, and I received the dubious honor of being introduced as the "Meat of the Week." Like "Hammer," it is kind of an offhanded compliment, as long as you can back it up.

On the water for the first time together, Mike is at stroke seat; I sit behind him at three, Harry at two, and Stormy at bow. Mike is easily six feet six inches tall, so I look forward to trying to match his reach. We row a couple of miles down river, throwing in "10's" and "20's" to test power and timing. Coming back we do more of the same, gradually increasing the rate to 36 strokes per minute on the final piece. There is a ton of power in this lineup. Raedene comments, "There is a lot of muscle in this boat. Maybe too much muscle. We need to smooth it out." Not that a pre-race row should be perfect. Keeping it a bit raw adds to the excitement. At the dock Mike puts it this way, "That felt like shit. We're going to do well tomorrow."

I arrive at Harvard's Newell boathouse sweating and thirsty. Fritz is testing the Olympic Silver medalists from the 1972 games. It is a jovial, carefree atmosphere. These guys have done this before. I ask if the fact that I have just been exercising will affect the outcome of my test. Fritz asks how much exercise and how long ago. I tell him that I just rowed about 8,000 meters then ran a mile to the boathouse with a backpack on. He hesitates for a split second before turning to his instruments of torture, "Get a drink of water. You'll do great."

The instruments for this test, a heart rate monitor and blood lactate measuring paraphernalia, aren't really torturous at all. This is a sub-max test, quite simple. I will row at a split of 1:57-1:58, around 210-220 watts, keeping my heart rate under 140 beats per minute or so, for 5 minutes. After 5 minutes Fritz will take a blood sample to measure blood lactate concentration. A measurement below 5.0 implies that your aerobic system is sufficiently developed so as not to be overpowered by your anaerobic system. A measurement above 5.0 implies that your aerobic system is not sufficiently developed. After each minute Marge records heart rate. Fritz says "You're doing great." At the end of the piece he draws blood from my finger - 3.8. Fritz pats me on the back, "Congratulations, you're in shape."

One of the men from the '72 Olympic 8+ is putting on his shirt. "Did he tell you that you were doing great?" I say yes. "He's been telling me that for 36 years. Just once, Fritz, I'd like to hear you tell me I'm doing lousy, just once!" Fritz responds, "All that matters are your numbers, and your numbers are good. Your life could be going down the tubes, but it doesn't matter because your numbers are good! Your stocks might be in the toilet, but you're doing great because the numbers say so!" This is hog heaven, the brass ring for a rowing numbers geek like me. I could do this all day. Sadly, with only so many hours in this day before the next one begins, I have to go. I give him a copy of my manuscript, we shake hands, and I am on my way. I catch the subway downtown. From where I sit, it feels more like a pony.

Saturday morning it is 37-38 degrees plus wind chill. Last year I had the flu and this race hurt a lot. I was definitely hanging from the dragon's tail in a blur of pain and delirium. This year I have successfully fended off a minor cold so I am ready to prove myself, to kick the dragon's tail, not hang from it. Today my demon has an entirely different face.

The Head of the Charles, as mentioned before, is a race against the clock. If you finish within 5% of the fastest time you are qualified to come back the following year. If you do not finish in the top 5% you enter a lottery to try to get back in – no guarantees. The Rocky Mountain boat finished 2nd last year and will start from that position this year. The winning boat, 1980 rowing club, is practically unbeatable. Knowing that, my most important job is to make sure that nobody beats us, to keep the 2nd place ranking. Because we all race the clock, a boat in 20th place could beat us and we would never even know it, possibly never even see them! I've never rowed, much less raced, with these guys. I am the untested Meat of the Week. They have asked me to row with them based on reputation and my association with Steve, who probably put in a good word for me. But Steve is not here now. For this go 'round I don't get to hide in his shadow. This is my truth, my undisputable reality - anything less than 2nd will be a failure. This is the face of my demon.

Like bulls at the gate we await the start. Nerves give way to excitement, excitement to aggression. Mike bangs the gunwales with his giant hands, like prehistoric man banging clubs as a show of force before battle. "Alright, let's do this thing." The beauty of the rolling start is that the transition is subtle. Before you know it, you're in it. Wilmington is 3rd at the start, San Diego 4th, and Pocock 5th. We are racing between 33 and 34 strokes per minute and Mike is definitely on his game. We have a good rhythm and I am ready as the pain tide floods. We are now well passed the "oh shit" moment and fully committed to the pain. By the first split at Riverside, we have a 9.548 second lead over Wilmington, 9.796 second lead over Pocock and a 15.876 lead over San Diego. What we don't know is that, way back in 16th place, Minneapolis Rowing is charging hard and trails by only 3.941 seconds. Mike and Stormy had warned us that Minneapolis would be "gunning for us." Their coxswain, John Jablonio, is a member of the Rocky Mountain Rowing Club.

The yellow pyramid shaped *one mile* marker does not congratulate me on finishing the first of three miles. The yellow pyramid shaped *one mile* marker mocks me, a crushing reminder that there are *two miles* left to go. Minneapolis is now 3.559 seconds behind us. I hear Harry's breath behind me, perfectly in sync with my own. That's something. Focus on that. We take two breaths per stroke, 66-68 breaths per minute. Saliva flies from my mouth and nose. Spitting would upset the rhythm. I am in control. I am having The Tammy Talk (with all I have invested in this sport, I want to be there for every stroke) in my head. My reality shifts. It is not that I have *only* completed one mile and have two long miles to go. It is that I have already completed one mile and I *only* have two miles left before this amazing experience is over! I begin to tear off giant chunks of pain and chew on them voraciously. The pain is empowering. It is my fuel. It is my friend.

This is so much better than last year. Raedene has developed a calm and steady pattern of alternating Power 10's; first for leg drive, then for length; then leg drive, then length. As a coach I used to tell my coxswains not to continuously repeat the same command, as it would desensitize the crew and dilute the command's intensity. But this is different. Raedene is not calling the same thing out of desperation, or because she doesn't know what else to say. Raedene knows exactly what she is doing. Raedene is a natural born killer.

Through the Powerhouse Stretch we swing and fly. I don't even remember seeing the *two mile* marker. At the Cambridge turn our lead over Minneapolis has increased to 4.520 seconds. All other boats are no longer in sight. We are alone, with 1980 somewhere ahead of us. Out of the Cambridge turn we begin our sprint at 37 strokes per minute. This is part of our race plan. Mike told me on the way to the starting line, "when I go, be ready to go with me." I am. He does. We all do. It is tremendous, vicious, primal. And then we are through. It is over.

Rocky Mountain Rowing Club maintains its' 2nd place ranking by 4.780 seconds over Minneapolis. Today, out of 26 boats, only Rocky Mountain and Minneapolis are fast enough to stay within 5% of the winning 1980 boat.

Walking along the riverbank I run into Chris Ives. We laugh at the crappy race his 8+ had. I tell him I'm writing a book, that he'll be in it. The funny thing is, this whole adventure really started eight years ago in Tacoma, Washington with the two of us talking about racing in San Diego! I owe so much to Steve for the opportunities that I have had. He has opened doors for me that I would never have gained access to on my own. That being said I needed this race. I needed to prove to Steve, and to myself, that when I show up, on my own, I can pull my weight. That is the face of today's demon, my demon, not to be mistaken with your demon, but maybe. I can now wear my "Meat of the Week" title proudly. **I have earned it.**

To see photos of this adventure visit our website:

racingyesterday.com